KINGDOM COME

The Kingdom Parables of Jesus in the Gospel of Matthew

KEN CLAYTON

KINGDOM COME

The Kingdom Parables of Jesus
in the Gospel of Matthew

Kingdom Come: The Kingdom Parables of Jesus in the Gospel of Matthew

ISBN 978-1-955295-52-9

COURIER PUBLISHING

100 Manly Street
Greenville, South Carolina 29601

PUBLISHED IN THE UNITED STATES OF AMERICA

DEDICATION

I want to dedicate this book to Joy, my wife and beloved co-worker in the gospel for over sixty years. I also want to dedicate this book to our daughter Jill, her husband Scott Dender, and their children: Grace, Joshua, Caleb, Elijah, Hannah, Josiah, and Luke; our son Kenny, his wife Sarah, and their children: Emily, Kenneth, John Cooper, and Ethan Wyatt.

FOREWORD

I was blessed to have Ken Clayton as my pastor for many years. Not only was he my spiritual advisor, he was a "good buddy" to me and my family. He and Joy (his wife) were two of the most loving people I have ever known. I found in him a fellow Christian who was a wonderful example of one who exemplified what it meant to be called a "child of God."

As a preacher, he opened God's Word effectively and dramatically. He proclaimed the truths of the Bible clearly so that the "common man" could understand — and in understanding, seek to follow the guidance of Jesus and the writers of the books of the Bible.

In two previous books written by Dr. Clayton, *The Key to Understanding the Gospel of John* and *Daniel: Courage in Chaos,* is evidence that he is an effective writer in explaining clearly the truths of those books. The same is true with this book, *Kingdom Come: The Kingdom Parables of Jesus in the Gospel of Matthew.*

Dr. Clayton guides the learner in exploring those kingdom parables that relate to everyday living for the Christian who wants to grow to be more like Jesus. Although the parable stories are from the time of Jesus on earth, the truths and guidance of the parables carry over to this century.

The structure of the chapters is in outline form, which makes it easy to follow the content. This form also is welcomed by those who will teach the book.

Mic Morrow
Retired Editor, Writer, and Consultant
Lifeway Christian Resources
Nashville, Tenn.

TABLE OF CONTENTS

INTRODUCTION

Jesus is the Master Storyteller. The parables of Jesus are memorable because they had a basis in everyday life, but they made a strong impact on the meaning that Jesus was putting forward. Someone has said that the parables are "earthly stories with a heavenly meaning." Usually Jesus was seeking to make His point with an illustration of that truth.

However, few of the first hearers of the parables understood them. Even the disciples asked Jesus, "Why do You speak to them in parables?" (Matt. 13:10). Jesus responded, "Therefore I speak to them in parables, because seeing they do not see, and hearing they do not hear, nor do they understand" (Matt. 13:13). Jesus went on to quote from Isaiah 6:9–10 to explain that just because people can physically see and hear does not mean that they are able to hear and see spiritual truths. The parables are more than interesting stories — because when people see the truth and live the truth, their lives are changed.

When Jesus finished the parable in Matthew 7:24–27 about "building on the rock," the people were "astonished at His teaching — for He taught them as one having authority, and not as the scribes" (Matt. 7:28–29). When the rabbis taught, they would quote what other rabbis had said or had written to support their position or interpretation. Jesus did not use or need that rabbinic method; He was His own authority. The people recognized the uniqueness of Jesus' teaching.

The Jews often used the phrase "kingdom of heaven," instead of using the name of God out of fear or respect. The "kingdom of heaven" was a Jewish way of saying the "kingdom of God." Matthew's gospel seems to have been written to appeal to a Jewish audience. Matthew discussed the law, the Sabbath, the temple, David, Moses, the Messiah, ceremonial law and many other terms and ideas familiar to the Jews. There are fifty-three

Old Testament references in Matthew. Matthew's goal, led by the Holy Spirit, was to prove to the Jews that Jesus was the promised Messiah and King.

Jesus' use of the "kingdom of heaven" points to the truth that His kingdom was a heavenly one. The expression "kingdom of heaven" is found in Matthew thirty-three times. Jesus did not come to restore the political fortunes of Israel. Jesus came to rule in the hearts of believers, beginning here on earth and continuing into eternity. In order to enter the kingdom, it is necessary to repent of sin and trust and obey Jesus as Lord and Savior.

The word "parable" comes from a compound word. One part originally meant "to lay or place." The other part meant "alongside of." Jesus took something familiar and placed a spiritual truth alongside it. If the hearers understood, it meant that their hearts and minds were open to Jesus and who He was.

Section I

Parables of the Kingdom

Parable of the Mustard Seed
Matthew 13:31–32

³¹"Another parable He put forth to them, saying: 'The kingdom of heaven is like a mustard seed, which a man took and sowed in his field, ³²which indeed is the least of all the seeds; but when it is grown it is greater than all the herbs and becomes a tree, so that the birds of the air come and nest in its branches.'"

Many years ago, my wife, Joy, and I were traveling through Israel with a tour group. Our guide stopped our tour bus by a tall-as-a-tree bush growing beside a narrow road just south of Jerusalem. We were able to see the tiny seeds from this mustard "tree."

The parable of the mustard seed reveals that before Jesus returns for His church, the number of people who are entering the kingdom (entering into a personal saving relationship with Jesus) will be very small at first. The church of the Lord Jesus would begin small, like the mustard seed, but would grow tremendously in comparison to its small beginnings.

CONTEXT

After hearing the parables of the sower and of the wheat and the tares, the disciples must have wondered how the kingdom of God would survive. People were rejecting Jesus, and others were planting evil seeds. The disciples must have wondered if Satan and the evil of this world would overwhelm the church.

Most of the Jewish leaders rejected Jesus as the Messiah. The multitude who followed Jesus were very shallow in their belief in Jesus. There was a small group, only twelve disciples, who remained constant in their fellowship with Jesus.

In the eyes of the world and perhaps His own disciples, the ministry of Jesus seemed insignificant. The world's perspective of the church has not changed. In the world's perspective, the church has little importance and influence. So today, how can the church have an impact on the vastly larger pagan world? Jesus would illustrate to His disciples that a handful of believers — weak and powerless in themselves, but with His power dwelling in them — would turn the world upside down. "Greater is He who is in you, than he who is in the world" (1 John 4:4).

THE PARABLE

In this parable, Jesus used the idea of planting a tiny seed that grew into tree size as an illustration of the growth of the kingdom of God. In verse 32, Jesus said it was the "least of all seeds." Some have rejected Jesus' comment, saying that mustard seed is not the smallest seed. Others have commented that it was the smallest seed that people in Jesus' day knew anything about. The real clue to Jesus' meaning is that the Greek word for "seed" used in verse 31 is always used for agricultural plants grown for food. Jesus was talking about seeds of garden plants in Israel. Mustard seed is the smallest of the food variety. There were wild, weed seeds that were smaller. Tobacco seeds are smaller, but tobacco was not grown in that part of the world until the sixteenth century or later. Of course, tobacco is sometimes chewed, but it is not a food crop!

Some people have been critical of Jesus talking about the size of the mustard plant — "... tree, and the birds of the air come and nest in its branches" (v. 32). But the mustard plant in Palestine often grows to twelve or fifteen feet tall.

The disciples did not need an explanation. The disciples understood. The kingdom of heaven was small, but it would one day grow into a large group of believers.

MEANING FOR US TODAY

First, the kingdom of God, the rule of the Lord, encourages us to be faithful, because the Lord will keep His promise that one day all nations will recognize His kingship. "Every knee shall bow and every tongue confess that Jesus Christ is Lord ..." (Phil. 2:9–11). Matthew used the other phrase "kingdom of heaven or kingdom of God" thirty-three times. Yes, Jesus shall reign!

Mary gave birth to Jesus in a stable, and He was placed in a manger for a bed. Jesus grew to manhood in Galilee, an insignificant part of the Roman Empire. When Nathaniel learned that Jesus was from Nazareth, he questioned, "Can any good thing come from Nazareth?" (John 1:46). The disciples were few in number, uneducated, fearful, weak and slow to understand. Yet the kingdom has grown. "The kingdoms of this world will become the kingdom of our Lord, and of His Christ, and He shall reign forever and ever" (Rev. 11:15).

Second, the kingdom of heaven will be a blessing to the rest of the world. The birds nesting in the tree is a symbol of safety and refuge for all who believe.

The kingdom will provide shelter, and will benefit the world. Christians throughout the years have been leaders in education, medicine, science, justice, human rights, and in many other ways.

Third, the battle belongs to the Lord. There is much opposition to the kingdom. Satan and his demons and the evil intentions of many people, stand against the kingdom of God. "He who is in you, is greater than he who is in the world" (1 John 4:4). In Jesus there is victory.

Fourth, the Lord alone measures what is significant. The Roman

Empire was powerful. Nazi Germany conquered Europe. The Berlin wall divided a city and nation. But the Roman Empire crumbled, Nazi Germany was defeated, and the Berlin wall was reduced to rubble. Empires rise and fall, but the church of the Lord Jesus remains! Jesus is King of kings and Lord of lords!

Fifth, the Lord grows His kingdom. Believers are called to be faithful, but it is the Lord who grows His kingdom. After Peter declared, "Thou art the Christ, the Son of the Living God," Jesus replied, "… On this rock I will build My church, and the gates of hell shall not prevail against it" (Matt. 16:16, 18).

Finally, the kingdom is here now. Jesus can rule in your heart when you open your life to Him. You may enter the kingdom today by faith in Jesus Christ as your Lord and Savior. Now when He was asked by the Pharisees when the kingdom of God would come, He answered them and said, "The kingdom of God does not come with observation, nor will they say, 'See here!' or 'See there!' For indeed, the kingdom of God is within you" (Luke 17:20–21).

Examine your own heart. If you are not obeying Jesus, following Jesus, serving Jesus or witnessing for Jesus, you have not truly trusted Jesus as your Lord and Savior and entered the kingdom of God. Jesus is coming again, but our first challenge is to enter the kingdom by faith in the Lord Jesus Christ!

Parable of the Leaven

Matthew 13:33

"Another parable He spoke to them: 'The kingdom of heaven is like leaven, which a woman took and hid in three measures of meal till it was all leavened.'"

Weddings are happy occasions. I have performed hundreds of wedding ceremonies over the years. In order to help young couples in our church, my wife, Joy, often organized and conducted bridal showers and wedding receptions. Of course, it is traditional to give wedding presents to the couple. That was true in New Testament times as well. When a Jewish girl was married, her mother gave her a small piece of dough from some prepared and baked just before the wedding. From this gift of leavened dough, the bride would bake bread for her family. This was a simple gift, but it represented the love of her family that would be a daily reminder to her.

In Matthew 13, Jesus was teaching that the kingdom of heaven is like leaven. Leaven was a common, ordinary substance, and the Jews might have been surprised that Jesus would compare heaven to leaven.

Leaven is produced when something becomes rotten. To the Jews in Jesus' day, leaven was often compared to something bad. Jesus even warned: "Beware of the leaven of the Pharisees" (Matt. 16:6). But in this parable, Jesus used leaven in a positive way.

The Setting of the Parable

In order to understand Jesus' use of leaven to explain the kingdom, we need to understand the bread-making process. There are two types of bread. One is leavened bread, and the other is unleavened bread. Unleavened bread was flat. The Jews were instructed by Moses to bake their bread hurriedly, not giving the dough time to rise with leaven. The deliverance from Egypt in bondage was celebrated every year with the Feast of Unleavened Bread and the Passover.

Bread was a staple food. Bread was baked every day. Remember, Jesus fed bread and fish to the five thousand (Matt. 14:13–21). In the model prayer that Jesus gave to His disciples, He taught them to pray: "Give us this day our daily bread" (Matt. 6:11).

Bread was prepared much like we prepare sourdough today. Wheat or barley (barley was cheaper) was ground by hand in a mortar and pestle, because grinding at a mill was expensive. For bread to rise, it must have an active ingredient. People would keep some of the dough from one batch in order to place it in the next batch of dough. The leaven would permeate the whole lump and make it rise when baked.

Earthly Story — Heavenly Meaning

Jesus said in the parable that a woman took leaven and "hid" it in the new batch of dough. It was "three measures" (Matt. 13:33), or a modern bushel. That was a large lump of dough! The primary function of leaven is to permeate the dough. The kingdom of heaven permeates all of you. Belonging to the kingdom will change you and, through you, change others.

What is the Meaning of the Parable?

What possible relevance could this brief parable have for us today? The vast majority of Americans buy bread already baked and packaged from the grocery store. I believe there are several important lessons Jesus will teach us from this brief parable.

Small things can have a great influence. The power of the kingdom is far greater than it may appear in the beginning. You may wonder, what can I do, or my church do, in the midst of a secular world that seems to be absorbed in evil? Yet, the truth of the kingdom of heaven is permeated with the power of the Holy Spirit. The influence of the kingdom is the influence of the King of kings and His word, the Bible.

In an obscure part of the world, in Galilee, Jesus started with twelve disciples, but the kingdom has grown and spread over the world.

In the parable, a little leaven permeated ten gallons of flour, enough bread to feed nearly two hundred people. The kingdom began small, but it is growing and it is powerful.

The influence of the kingdom comes from within the believer's heart. The leaven was "hid in three measures of meal …" (Matt. 13:33). Just as leaven works within the dough with visible results, the kingdom works on the heart and mind of believers in Jesus to produce visible changes in behavior. When the kingdom of God is reflected in our lives, its influence invades the world. You don't have to be a prominent person to influence the world around you. Just be faithful to the Lord. Jesus prayed for His disciples: "They are not of the world, just as I am not of the world. … As you sent Me into the world, I also have sent them into the world" (John 17:16, 18).

The kingdom is to be passed on. "Therefore, we also, since we are surrounded by so great a cloud of witnesses, let us lay aside every weight, and the sin which so easily ensnares us, and let us run with endurance the race that is set before us, looking unto Jesus, the author and finisher of our faith …" (Heb. 12:1–2). In view of all that was written about the faithful followers of the Lord in Hebrews 11, we are called to run our race through life and keep our eyes on Jesus.

We don't stand alone. We follow in the line of believers, martyrs, Christian teachers, and preachers of the past. We must take a piece of the leaven of the kingdom and pass it on to the next generation.

Each believer has a purpose. Just as leaven had the purpose of making the dough rise, so believers have the purpose of knowing Christ and making Him known. I have used that statement in the last four churches I have pastored. The Great Commission found in Matthew 28:19–20 is not a suggestion, but a command. If your goal is to just coast into heaven on your good works, you are not living as leaven in the world.

The kingdom will come. Just as Jesus taught us to pray, "Your kingdom come …" (Matt. 6:10), we know that in His timing the kingdom will be established and be victorious. Jesus wanted His disciples and us to know that not only would His kingdom grow and prosper, but would conquer evil and Jesus will reign as King of kings and Lord of lords. "… Alleluia! For the Lord God Omnipotent reigns! Let us be glad and rejoice and give Him glory, for the marriage of the Lamb has come, and His wife (the church) has made herself ready" (Rev. 19:6–7).

We began, and we will close, this study of the parable about leaven with the beautiful concept of marriage. Marriage is a symbol of the close relationship between believers and the Lord Jesus. Will you be present at the marriage supper of the Lamb? (Rev. 19:9).

Parable of the Hidden Treasure and the Pearl of Great Price

Matthew 13:44–46

[44]"Again, the kingdom of heaven is like treasure hidden in a field, which a man found and hid; and for joy over it he goes and sells all that he has and buys that field."
[45]"Again, the kingdom of heaven is like a merchant seeking beautiful pearls. [46]"Who, when he had found one pearl of great price, went and sold all that he had and bought it."

What is your favorite sport? What is the highest award for your favorite sport? If, for you, it is tennis, winning at Wimbledon would be an honor. If it is professional football, it would be winning the Super Bowl. If it is golf, it would be receiving the green jacket at the Masters. It could be winning a gold medal in an Olympic event. How do these athletes win these championships? They determine what their goal is and they commit their all to achieve that goal. Paul wrote: "I press on toward the goal for the prize of the upward call of God in Christ Jesus" (Phil. 3:14).

Jesus told two parables with the same main idea. The parable about the hidden treasure in the field and the parable about a valuable pearl make the point that when a person discovers the most valuable thing, that person sells all he has to obtain what is most valuable.

THE PARABLE OF THE HIDDEN TREASURE

This parable sounds strange to us, but it was a common practice in Palestine. Most people used the ground as their bank. There is a Rabbinic saying: "One safe place for your money, the earth."

During the American Civil War, Southerners would often hide valuables in the ground to conceal them from marauders or soldiers. Palestine was one of the most fought-over areas in the world. So it was a common practice to try to protect valuables by hiding them in the ground. Later, if someone else found the hidden treasure, it was "finders, keepers."

In the parable, a man was working in a field and discovered a treasure. The man was filled with joy and excitement and sold all he had in order to buy that field.

WHAT DOES THE PARABLE MEAN?

Do you remember the joy you felt when you first accepted Christ as your Savior? Do you remember the feelings of knowing your sin was forgiven and your destination was your eternal home in heaven? Jesus wanted His hearers to know the joy of finding and entering into the kingdom.

Jesus was also teaching that the kingdom is worth any sacrifice you have to make in order to enter. The man in the parable sold everything he had to purchase the field that contained the treasure.

THE PARABLE OF THE PEARL OF GREAT PRICE

In the ancient world, pearls were very valuable. Pearls were valued for their beauty and the high price they would bring when sold. Pearls were only found in the Red Sea and in the waters around England in those days. To realize the value of pearls, John in the Book of Revelation had a vision of the new Jerusalem, "descending out of heaven from God" (Rev. 21:10). Later, John described the gates of the city: "The twelve gates were twelve pearls: each individual gate was one pearl" (Rev. 21:21).

In this parable, a merchant was searching for beautiful pearls for resale. One day he found the most beautiful pearl he had ever seen. The pearl was very expensive, but the merchant sold all that he had and bought it.

WHAT DOES THE PARABLE MEAN?

There are many pearls, but there is only one best pearl. There are many worthy activities, many good and helpful causes. The question is, "What is God's best for me?" The only way to discover true peace, joy and hope is to commit your life to following Jesus and discover the will of God for your life.

Again, Jesus was teaching that in order to enter the kingdom, it is worth the loss of everything else in life. Entering the kingdom should be our top priority.

WHAT CAN BE LEARNED FROM THESE TWO PARABLES?

We should give up everything to gain the greatest thing of value — that is, entering the kingdom of our Lord Jesus Christ. We must take up our cross and follow Jesus (Matt. 16:24). Do you really want to be a part of the kingdom badly enough to give up everything to follow the Lord Jesus Christ?

What is your treasure? "Treasure" indicates those things or persons who have your greatest allegiance.

The treasure was "hidden" (v. 44). God's plan of grace, forgiveness, and salvation through the death of His only begotten Son on the cross and His burial and resurrection was once hidden, but has been revealed. "In Him, we have redemption through His blood, the forgiveness of sins, according to the riches of His grace which He made to abound toward us in all wisdom and prudence, having made known to us the mystery of His will, according to His good pleasure which He purposed in Himself ..." (Eph. 1:7–9).

The greatest goal in life is to enter the kingdom. In both parables, the individuals sold everything in order to possess the prize. Jesus declared: "Seek first the kingdom of God and His righteousness and all these things shall be added to you" (Matt. 6:33). We must stay focused on the kingdom of God. You can only have one number one priority. No halfway measures will work. You are either all in or all out.

Jesus gave up everything to come to this earth to redeem all who would respond in faith to Him. Jesus decided to die on a cross to pay the penalty for our sin. Jesus "redeemed" us or "bought us out of slavery." *"Christ has redeemed us …" (Gal. 3:13). "For you were bought (redeemed) with a price" (1 Cor. 6:20). "… to redeem those who were under the law, that we might receive the adoption as sons" (Gal. 4:5).* Jesus paid the greatest price to redeem us from sin and bring us home because He loves us so much. Will you respond to the love of Jesus and follow Him as your Lord and Savior? Will you be willing to give up everything to enter the kingdom?

Parable of the Unforgiving Servant
Matthew 18:21–35

[22]*"Jesus said to him, 'I do not say to you, up to seven times, but up to seventy times seven. *[23]*Therefore the kingdom of heaven is like a certain king who wanted to settle accounts with his servants. *[24]*And when he had begun to settle accounts, one was brought to him who owes him ten thousand talents. *[25]*But as he was not able to pay, his master commanded that he be sold, with his wife and children and all that he had, and that payment should be made. *[26]*The servant therefore fell down before him, saying, 'Master, have patience with me, and I will pay you all.' *[27]*Then the master of that servant was moved with compassion, released him, and forgave him the debt.*

[28]*But that servant went out and found one of his fellow servants who owed him a hundred denarii, and he laid hands on him and took him by the throat saying, 'Pay me what you owe!' *[29]*So his fellow servant fell down at his feet and begged him saying, 'Have patience with me, and I will pay you all.' *[30]*And he would not, but went and threw him into prison till he should pay the debt. *[31]*So when his fellow servants saw what had been done, they were very grieved and came and told their master all that had been done. *[32]*Then his master, after he had called him, said to him, 'You wicked servant! I forgave you all that debt because*

you begged me. ³³*Should you not also have had compassion on your fellow servant just as I had pity on you?* ³⁴*His master was angry, and delivered him to the torturers until he should pay all that was due to him.* ³⁵*So My heavenly Father also will do to you if each of you, from his heart, does not forgive his brother his trespasses."*

There are so many broken homes and broken relationships because of a lack of forgiveness. Our human tendency is to seek revenge or get even with someone for a wrong done to us. Do you have an attitude of unforgiveness toward another person? Is that person a member of your own family?

Over the years working with young couples in premarital counseling, I have encouraged young men with this old saying: "If Mama ain't happy, then nobody is happy!" So I encourage the young men to take the initiative and apologize. We all must seek forgiveness and be forgiving if we are to continue in relationships with other people. Jesus taught His disciples in His model prayer to pray: "And forgive us our debts, as we forgive our debtors" (Matt. 5:12).

Jesus told a powerful parable about forgiveness. This parable is easy to read but difficult to practice in our daily lives.

Context

In the 18th chapter of Matthew, verses 15–17, Jesus gave instructions about how to mend a broken relationship with a fellow believer who has sinned against you. You are to go and talk with that person first. If he refuses to hear you, take one or two others to talk with him. If that fails, then take it to the church. That could cause the person to realize their sin, repent, and be restored to the fellowship.

Peter then approached Jesus with a question. "How many times must

I forgive?" (Matt. 18:21). Rabbinical rules required that you forgive three times. Peter must have felt he was being generous by offering to forgive seven times. Jesus responded: "Not seven but seventy times seven" (Matt. 18:22). Forgiveness should have no boundaries.

THE PARABLE OF THE UNFORGIVING SERVANT

The parable is the simple story of a servant who owed his master an incredible amount of money. A talent was a weight of gold or silver. Ten thousand talents could amount to millions of dollars today. The king wanted to settle accounts, but the servant was not able to pay. So the king commanded that the servant sell his family, and all he owned to pay the debt (Matt. 18:24–25). So the servant fell down before the king and begged for more time to pay the debt. The king was moved with compassion and forgave the entire debt (Matt. 18:27).

However, when this servant left the king, he encountered a fellow servant that owed him one hundred denarii. A denarius was a day's wages for an ordinary worker. This debtor pleaded with the fellow servant with the same pleas the first servant had used with the king (Matt. 18:26). But the second servant was not forgiven, and instead was thrown into prison until he could repay the debt.

The third section of the parable begins when some other servants learned of this injustice and reported it to the king (Matt. 18:31). The king told that wicked servant: "Should you not have had compassion?" Then the king delivered the wicked servant to the tormentors until he paid the debt.

In verse 35, Jesus declared the point of the parable: "So My heavenly Father also will do to you if each of you, from his heart, does not forgive his brother his trespasses."

THE MEANING OF THE PARABLE FOR US TODAY

We must forgive in order to be forgiven. In the parable, the wicked servant would not forgive his fellow worker. Jesus said: "Blessed are the merciful for they shall obtain mercy" (Matt. 5:7). In explaining a portion of the Lord's model prayer to the disciples, Jesus said: "For if you forgive men their trespasses, your heavenly Father will also forgive you" (Matt. 6:14). The Lord's forgiveness given to us must be passed on to those who offend us.

Our forgiveness of others is based on God's great forgiveness of our overwhelming sin debt. In the parable, the contrast between the two debts is staggering. It would take a herd of donkeys to carry the weight of gold that amounted to millions of dollars. The one hundred denarii debt could be carried by one man! Whatever wrong you have ever suffered does not compare to the great sin debt that the Lord has forgiven you. Our sin debt is beyond our ability to pay. Our sin put Jesus on the cross. Even on the cross, Jesus prayed: "Father, forgive them, for they know not what they do." We forfeit God's forgiveness when we refuse to forgive others.

Unforgiveness leads to hell. In the parable, Jesus said: "His master was angry, and delivered him to the torturers until he should pay all that was due to him" (Matt. 18:34). This demonstrates how vital forgiveness is if we are to have a relationship with Jesus. Jesus then told His hearers that His heavenly Father would do exactly the same to them, if they did not forgive. Jesus said, "From your hearts" (Matt. 18:35). I believe that means that you really forgive and forget and not hold a grudge.

This is an area where we need to examine our hearts. If we harbor hatred and unforgiveness in our hearts, it is a sign that we have never truly been saved.

On the cross in mercy and compassion, Jesus made forgiveness available to all people who come to Him in repentance and faith. But if there is no true repentance and faith, judgment and hell will follow (Matt. 18:34–35).

Forgiveness is an act of love. "For God so loved the world, that He gave His only begotten Son …" (John 3:16). God loves us and gave His Son to die on the cross for our sins. When you realize that God's amazing grace and love has forgiven you, then you will be able to forgive others. But if you are not walking in the grace of the Lord and you have forgotten all that He has forgiven you, you will not show love and forgiveness to others.

Be honest. Examine your heart. Are you harboring unforgiveness toward someone? Confess it to Jesus. Then determine to speak to that person, or call them or write a letter to them expressing your forgiveness and seeking their forgiveness for yourself. If that person is no longer living, repent to the Lord and forgive that person. Let go of your grudge and be free. Jesus offers us forgiveness and we must offer the same to others. Forgiveness is an essential ingredient to kingdom living.

Parable of the Great Shepherd
Matthew 18:10–14

[10]"Take heed that you do not despise one of these little ones, for I say to you that in heaven their angels always see the face of My Father who is in heaven. [11]For the Son of Man has come to save that which was lost."

[12]"What do you think? If a man has a hundred sheep, and one of them goes astray, does he not leave the ninety-nine and go to the mountains to seek the one who is straying? [13]And if he should find it, assuredly, I say to you, he rejoices more over that sheep than over the ninety-nine that did not go astray. [14]Even so it is not the will of your Father who is in heaven that one of these little ones should perish."

What is your first reaction when you hear of a new plan of operation at your work or your school, or from the government: Is it, "How will this affect me?" or "What's in it for me?" Is that your type of response? Many people, when given an opportunity to enter the kingdom of God, may have similar reactions. The question "What will I get out of it?" is the way the disciples responded to Jesus' teaching about the kingdom.

Mohammed Ali, the heavyweight world champion boxer, used to say that he was the "greatest." Many people aspire to be great. After all that is what elections and athletic contests try to decide. How would you describe greatness? You might say someone who has reached the highest point of their profession. Perhaps you would name some famous politicians, world champion athletes or successful movie stars. After a discussion about greatness among His disciples, Jesus told a parable of one lost sheep in Matthew 18:10–14. In order to understand the parable an examination of the first part of chapter 18 in Matthew is necessary.

CONTEXT

The disciples had been arguing about who would be the greatest in the kingdom. Finally, they asked Jesus to settle the question. We know that today, that kind of selfishness can infect a church and destroy the fellowship instead of building up the kingdom. For Jesus, this was a teachable moment, this selfish attitude needed to be corrected before more damage could be done.

The teaching of Jesus was not only characterized by the use of parables but, on this occasion by "show and tell." Jesus took a little child (Matt. 18:2) as an example. Jesus taught that a person had to be "converted" (Matt. 18:3), which means totally changed. A person's heart must be committed to Jesus and not the world. "Assuredly, I say to you, unless you are converted and become as little children, you will by no means enter the kingdom of heaven" (Matt. 18:3). So then Jesus made His point with the disciples, that the greatest in the kingdom are those who are humble. On another occasion, Jesus told Nicodemus that in order to enter the kingdom that he must be "born-again" (John 3:3). We must be humble and dependent upon our heavenly Father as a child is to their parents.

THE SEEKING SHEPHERD

Immediately before beginning His parable, Jesus drove home His point about children. No one should despise or harm a child because "in heaven their angels always see the face of My Father who is in heaven" (Matt. 18:10). What a wonderful truth Jesus gave us. True believers, children of God, have angels that always have immediate access to our heavenly Father! Do you believe in angels? You should. Jesus has appointed angels to watch over His children.

Jesus also made it clear what His purpose on earth was: "For the Son of Man has come to save that which was lost" (Matt. 18:11). Jesus came to save those who are spiritually lost and who, without Jesus, will spend eternity in hell. Jesus also wants to encourage believers who have lost their purpose, forgotten their first love, or strayed from Him. So Jesus told the disciples this parable about the Great Shepherd seeking one lost sheep.

THE PARABLE

As the master teacher, Jesus wanted to engage His disciples in the story by asking: "What do you think?" (Matt. 18:12). Jesus said that a shepherd with one hundred sheep had one that went astray. So the shepherd went off to find that one sheep. When the shepherd found the lost sheep, he rejoiced over that one "more" than the ninety-nine who were safe (Matt. 18:13). Jesus made it abundantly clear what is the perfect will of the Father, "that not one of these little ones should perish" (Matt. 18:14).

I have read that sheep are helpless creatures. They needed a shepherd to guide them to pasture and water and protect them from wild animals (read Psalm 23). Lost sheep tend to walk in circles, never finding their own way home. It was easy for sheep to go astray in the hills of Judea. A ridge-like narrow plateau runs north and south through Judea. There are many ravines on both sides of the plateau and pastureland is sparse. Years ago a shepherd was looking for a lost sheep in the rugged Qumran area, when he discovered biblical scrolls in a cave, later called the Dead Sea Scrolls. Shepherds were experts in tracking their sheep. Jesus is the Great Shepherd seeking lost sheep. Jesus said: "I am the good shepherd. The good shepherd gives His life for the sheep"; "I am the good shepherd, and I know My sheep, and am known by My own" (John 10:11, 14).

Meaning for Today

The love of Jesus is an individual love. The shepherd went after the one who was lost. The phrase "goes astray" in verse 12 could be translated "led astray." What if this is one of the little ones who might be "harmed" (Matt. 18:6) or "despised" (Matt. 18:10)? Jesus, like a good shepherd, searches to find lost sheep.

The love of Jesus is a patient love. Remember, when sheep become separated from the shepherd they will wander in circles til the shepherd finds them or they die. Of course, the sheep would have no one to blame but themselves for the trouble they may encounter! We are the sheep! In order to survive, we must be with the Shepherd, the Lord Jesus Christ. Even though we are foolish, Jesus loves us, and He is searching to find us. The shepherd did not wait to see if the sheep would come back, he went to find it. It is difficult for some to understand that not only will God forgive us when we come before Him in repentance, but the Lord takes the initiative to search for us.

The love of Jesus is a perfect love. Human "love" can be dominating, oppressive, controlling, harsh, distant, and thoughtless. But Jesus' love is demonstrated by the truth that He wants what is best for us. Jesus wants to protect us, and fill us with joy, peace, and hope. His desire is for us to be pure and holy.

The love of Jesus is a rejoicing love. The shepherd rejoiced "more" over finding the one lost sheep than he did the ninety-nine sheep who were safe. Jesus explained: "… there will be more rejoicing in heaven over one sinner who repents than over ninety-nine (that did not go astray)." Jesus' parable ended in a joyful celebration. How do you treat people who have wronged you and later asked for forgiveness? Do you have an attitude of contempt, or hold a grudge or give them a lecture? We are prone to say we forgive, but we often do not forget. But when the Lord forgives, He says, "Their sins I will remember no more" (Jer. 31:34).

A true child of God never loses his salvation, but we may remove ourselves from the love and fellowship of fellow believers and grow cold to the mission and task that the Lord has called us to perform. One of the common ways of separating ourselves from the power of the Holy Spirit working in us, is to become selfishly concerned about who is the greatest.

Are you worried about who is the greatest? "Now may the God of peace who brought up our Lord Jesus from the dead, that great Shepherd of the sheep, through the blood of the everlasting covenant, make you complete in every good work to do His will …" (Heb. 13:20–21). Remember, Jesus is great; we are the sheep!

Parable of the Workers in the Vineyard
Matthew 20:1-16

¹"For the kingdom of heaven is like a landowner who went out early in the morning to hire laborers for the vineyard. ²Now when he had agreed with the laborers for a denarius a day; he sent them into his vineyard. ³And he went out about the third hour and saw others standing idle in the marketplace, ⁴and said to them, 'You also go into the vineyard, and whatever is right I will give you.' So they went. ⁵Again he went out about the sixth and ninth hour, and did likewise. ⁶And about the eleventh hour he went out and found others standing idle and said to them, 'Why have you been standing here idle all day?' ⁷They said to him, 'Because no one hired us.' He said to them, 'You also go into the vineyard, and whatever is right you will receive.' ⁸So when evening had come, the owner of the vineyard said to his steward, 'call the laborers and give them their wages, beginning with the last to the first. ⁹And when those came who were hired about the eleventh hour, they each received a denarius. ¹⁰But when the first came, they supposed that they would receive more; and they likewise received a denarius. ¹¹And when they had received it, they complained against the landowner, ¹²saying, 'These *last men have worked only an hour, and you made them equal to us who, have borne the burden and the heat of the day. ¹³But he answered one of them and said, "Friend, I am doing you no wrong. Did you not agree with me for a denarius? ¹⁴Take what is yours and go your way. I wish to give to this last man the same as to you. ¹⁵Is it not lawful for me to do what I wish with my own things? Or is your eye evil because I am good? ¹⁶So the last will be first, and the first last. For many are called, but few chosen."*

CONTEXT

Jesus gave the parable of the workers in the vineyard as a response to Peter's question: "See, we have left all and followed You. Therefore what shall we have?" (Matt. 19:27). Peter was concerned about his place in the future kingdom. He wanted to know his reward for his service. Jesus could have rebuked Peter for this selfish question, but instead, Jesus revealed that these first disciples would reign with Him (Matt. 19:28–29). The main point Jesus made then and in the parable of the workers in the vineyard is: "But many who are first will be last, and the last first" (Matt. 19:30 and Matt. 20:16).

Those who may achieve high esteem for their service while on earth, may be humbled in heaven. Those who humbly and quietly served on earth may be lifted higher in heaven. The judgment of the Lord is not man's judgment.

One day Jesus was sitting in the temple area in Jerusalem near the treasury observing those who were making their donations. Jesus saw a poor widow put in two mites. Jesus said: "Truly I say to you that this poor widow has put in more than all; for all those out of their abundance have put in offering for God, but she out of her poverty put in all the livelihood that she had" (Luke 21:3–4).

Jesus not only sees our actions, He knows our hearts.

THE PARABLE

In the parable of the workers in the vineyard, Jesus is comparing service in the kingdom of God to the common practice of hiring day laborers to help gather the grape harvest. The grape harvest occurred toward the end of September. The fall rains came in our months of October and November. If the grapes were not gathered before the rains came, they would be ruined. The harvest had to be done very quickly. It was a race against the weather. Therefore, the landowner needed as many workers as he could find.

A denarius was the wage for a working man for one day's work. That amount would be needed to provide food for the worker's family for that day. Day laborers were the lowest class of workers. They were not attached to a family's estate like slaves and servants. So long as their master's situation was good, slaves and servants were in no danger of starvation. But a day laborer was on his own. If they were unemployed even for one day their children could go hungry. These day laborers were desperate for work.

When I was a young pastor attending seminary, I pastored a church in a rural farming area. It was a common practice for farm owners to go to town early in the morning to find laborers to help harvest tobacco or cut and bale hay. Workers would gather near the Farmers Co-op building in town hoping to find work during harvest times.

The hours mentioned in the parable are the normal Jewish hours. The Jewish twenty-four-hour day began at 6 p.m. to the following 6 p.m. Sunrise was at 6 a.m. So counting forward, the third hour is 9 a.m., the sixth hour is twelve noon, and the eleventh hour is 5 p.m.

This parable presented the familiar picture of life in a Jewish village at harvest time, when extra laborers were needed to gather the grape harvest before the rains came. The landowner kept going to the village to hire additional laborers. The surprise twist to this parable of Jesus was that the landowner paid all the workers the same even though some only worked one hour.

The Meaning of The Parable

Jesus was warning the Jews. The Jews were the chosen people of God. They had been chosen to be His witnesses to the world (Isaiah 43:10–12). However, most of them had failed in that mission. Most often, they hated the Gentiles or looked down on them. Jesus wanted the Jews to realize that God was gathering others to come into the kingdom and instead of being rebellious and resenting the Gentiles they should have received them.

Jesus was warning the disciples. The disciples were the first to know Jesus and to hear His teaching. Yet, as time would go on, others would enter the kingdom. As with Peter (Matt. 19:27), they would all need to love and receive all who enter the kingdom as fellow believers in Christ.

I have known some people who were longtime members of a church or charter members of a church who resented new people who joined and were asked to be in leadership roles. All who are in Christ are part of the family of God whether they come into the church early in life or later in life.

The Meaning of The Parable for Us Today

Besides Jesus' main point in this parable, it also has other truths that apply to us today.

Hope. The parable demonstrates the truth that whether you enter the kingdom as a youth or in your old age, you are precious to the Lord. So no matter when you come to faith in Jesus as your Lord and Savior, Jesus is waiting for you in love to welcome you home. Our hope is based on the love and forgiveness of Jesus.

Love. In the parable, desperate men were waiting for opportunities to work. The landowner, out of compassion, hired some at the last hour and also paid them a day's wages. That illustrates the generous love of the Lord for all who come to Him.

Grace. All that Jesus gives to us demonstrates His grace toward us.

In the parable, the last workers did not earn a day's wage. They did not deserve a day's wage. What the Lord gives us is not pay, it is a gift. We cannot earn nor do we deserve the forgiveness of God or a home in heaven. Yet in His abundant mercy and grace, Jesus offers us these gifts.

Service. Remember, Peter asked basically: "What do we get out of it?" If your reason for service to the kingdom is solely based on your future position or reward, your heart is in the wrong place. We should serve out of a sense of gratitude for all the Lord has done for us. In the parable, the workers were surprised that the last workers were grateful for any amount to help feed their family. I believe they would have been overjoyed at this generous gift. Do you have a heart of gratitude to the Lord?

Urgency. In the parable, the landowner knew his grapes had to be harvested before the rains came. We also should have a sense of urgency about the harvest of souls for the kingdom. Time is short, because life is short. We need to witness for Christ while we have the opportunity. Jesus said: "I must work the works of Him who sent Me while it is day; the night is coming when no one can work" (John 9:4).

A question we must all answer is: Am I truly working for the kingdom of God?

Section II
Parables on the Rejection of the Kingdom

BUILDING ON THE ROCK
MATTHEW 7:21–27

[21]"Not everyone who says to Me, 'Lord, Lord', shall enter the kingdom of heaven, but he who does the will of My Father in heaven. [22]Many will say to Me in that day, 'Lord, Lord, have we not prophesied in Your name, cast out demons in Your name, and done many wonders in Your name?' [23]And then I will declare to them, 'I never knew you; depart from Me, you who practice lawlessness!'

[24]"Therefore whoever hears these saying of mine, and does them, I will liken him to a wise man who built his house on the rock: [25]and the rain descended, the floods came, and the winds blew and beat on that house, and it did not fall, for it was founded on the rock.

[26]"But everyone who hears these saying of Mine, and does not do them, will be like a foolish man who built his house on the sand: [27]and the rain descended, the floods came, and the winds blew and beat on that house; and it fell. And great was its fall."

The parable contracts wise and foolish builders. Of course, a good foundation is essential for any building to stand. The famous leaning Tower of Pisa is one hundred seventy-nine feet tall and was built in 1173. It has leaned one twentieth of an inch every year and is now seventeen feet out of plumb! Several years ago concrete was poured into the ground to stabilize the tower. "Pisa" means "marshy land" and the foundation is only ten feet deep. It was built on a faulty foundation. This parable of Jesus is about two builders, two houses, two foundations and two different results.

THE HISTORICAL SETTING OF THE PARABLE

Notice the first word in Matthew 7:24 is "Therefore." This refers back to what Jesus had declared to the people recorded in Matthew 7:21–23. There are many people who claim to know Jesus and say they are His followers (Matt. 7:21). However, Jesus explained that the person who "does the will of My Father in heaven" is the one who will enter the kingdom of heaven. Prior to that, Jesus had stated: "A good tree cannot bear bad fruit, nor can a bad tree bear good fruit. … Therefore by their fruits you shall know them" (Matt. 7:18, 20). So in the context of Jesus teaching about how people were responding to the preaching of the kingdom, Jesus taught the people a parable about a wise builder and a foolish builder.

THE PARABLE

These builders had some things in common.

Both builders heard the words of Jesus: "Therefore whoever hears these sayings of Mine …" (Matt. 7:24, 26).

Both builders build similar houses. There are no differences described by Jesus in the two houses.

A very severe storm hit both houses (Matt. 7:25, 27). These builders also had some differences.

The first builder built his house upon the rock (Matt. 7:24). The word "rock" can mean "bedrock." The man must have dug down to bedrock to build his house on a firm foundation. This man represents those people who hear the gospel and build their lives on Jesus.

The second builder built his house on sand. This showed little planning and little wisdom. Sand is unstable and changing. In the news recently, a sinkhole opened in the sandy soil of Florida and swallowed two houses.

A severe storm struck both houses (Matt. 7:25, 27). The dry, desert areas of Palestine are crisscrossed with wadis. These dry depressions in the ground can become flooded with water in the rainy seasons. The results were disastrous for the person who built his house on the sand.

What is the Meaning of the Parable?

In the parable, the rains came, the floods followed, and the winds blew. This is the image of judgment. There were two houses, representing two ways of life. The storm of judgment came. The house on sand was destroyed. No hope, dreams, plans, efforts, or work could save this house. This will happen to any person who builds his life on anything but Jesus Christ.

Jesus was talking to religious people who thought their works, their self-righteous deeds, were enough to offer to God. They were building their religion on the sand of good works. We must be in a faith relationship with the Lord Jesus Christ. John wrote: "He that hath the Son hath life; and he that hath not the Son of God hath not life" (1 John 5:12).

The house, the life, built on the rock experienced the same storm. The rain, the flood, the wind "beat upon" the house (v. 25). The house was battered, but it stood against the storm. It did not fall, because this house or life was on a firm foundation. That true firm foundation is the Lord Jesus Christ.

Truths for Today

Your life must be based on a faith relationship with the Lord Jesus Christ. If our life is grounded in work, in politics, goals, or achievements, it will fail. Our lives may look sturdy to us and to others, but these foundations will not survive the judgment of God. Jesus said, "And great was the fall of it" (Matt. 7:27). A life without Jesus will totally fail.

If your life is built on the Rock of the Lord Jesus Christ, you will overcome every storm safe in the arms of Jesus.

Do you have Jesus Christ as the foundation of your life? "Neither is there salvation in any other: for there is no other name under heaven given among men, whereby we must be saved" (Acts 4:12).

Are you building your life on the Rock of Jesus Christ? If not, come to Jesus. Trust Him as your Lord and Savior. The great storm is coming. Will you spiritually survive the storm?

Paul wrote to the church in Corinth: "For we are God's fellow workers; you are God's field, you are God's building. According to the grace of God which was given to me, as a wise master builder I have laid the foundation, and another builds on it. But to each one take heed how he builds on it. For no other foundation can anyone lay than that which is laid, which is Jesus Christ" (1 Cor. 3:9–11).

Jesus Questioned About Fasting

Matthew 9:14–17

[14]"Then the disciples of John came to Him, saying, 'Why do we and the Pharisees fast often, but Your disciples do not fast?' [15]And Jesus said to them, 'Can the friends of the bridegroom mourn as long as the bridegroom is with them? But the days will come when the bridegroom will be taken away from them, and then they will fast.' [16]No one puts a piece of unshrunk cloth on an old garment; for the patch pulls away from the garment, and the tear is made worse. [17]Nor do they put new wine into old wineskins or else the wineskins break, the wine is spilled, and the wineskins are ruined. But they put new wine into new wineskins, and both are preserved."

An old saying that is associated with weddings is that the bride should have "something old, something new, something borrowed, something blue." When Jesus was questioned about why His disciples did not fast, Jesus referred to the joy of the friends of the bridegroom at a wedding (Matt. 9:15) Jesus went on to explain he was bringing something "new" (Matt. 9:16–17).

Teaching can be boring or it can be interesting. Jesus never bored people when He taught. Some hearers marveled, some were angered, but no one was bored! When questioned about fasting, Jesus did not give a long lecture about fasting. Jesus did not present a long speech about how to repair their old religious system and replace it with His revolutionary new truth. Instead Jesus told them a brief three-part parable.

Context

- This parable came at the end of three events of conflict with religious leaders.
- Jesus forgave the sins of a paralytic man and upset the scribes (Matt. 9:1–8).
- Jesus was eating in Matthew's home with other tax collectors and sinners which angered the Pharisees (Matt. 9:9–13).
- Jesus did not promote frequent fasting. Fasting was required by the Scriptures only on the Day of Atonement. The disciples of John the Baptist were critical of Jesus because of this (Matt. 9:14–17).

The Response

Remember, as someone has said, "A parable is an earthly story with a heavenly meaning." Jesus responded to His critics by a series of parabolic illustrations. Jesus began with the question about fasting by using the illustration of a wedding.

The bridegroom is present. The disciples of John the Baptist were continuing to prepare the way for the coming of the Messiah. But the Messiah had come! "Can the friends of the bridegroom mourn as long as the bridegroom is with them?" (Matt. 9:15).

A wedding was the most joyous occasion for any family. So it was a time to celebrate with the bridegroom, instead of being sad and fasting.

When John baptized Jesus, the Holy Spirit came as a dove and landed on Jesus. The voice of the Father declared, "This is My beloved Son in whom I am well pleased" (Matt. 3:17). John and his disciples should have been convinced that Jesus was the Messiah and they did not have to look for another. They were fasting and missing out on the wedding feast. They were more on the side of the Pharisees than on the side of Jesus.

Jesus could have asked, "Why are you more interested in the outward ritual of fasting than on the inward relationship with me?" What about you and me? Are we more interested in the form of religion or the true faith in Jesus? Are we more caught up in the latest religious books, or programs, or training themes or rituals than we are interested in a closer intimacy with Jesus? Our heart's desire should be to be more like Jesus, to be more filled with the awe of His presence than to spend our time admiring the physical trappings of religion.

Jesus didn't come to repair religion. "No one puts a piece of unshrunk cloth on an old garment; for the patch pulls away from the garment, and the tear is made worse" (Matt. 9:16).

In our modern times there is a process called "sanforizing." This process preshrinks cloth. So a new fabric can be used to patch an older garment today. But in biblical times, if you patched a garment with new cloth, it would pull away from the old garment as it would shrink when washed. Jesus said, "The tear is made worse."

Jesus did not come to patch up Judaism, nor to patch up some misunderstandings in their form of religion. Jesus was bringing a new revelation of God, not patching an old religion. Jesus won't patch up your worldly lifestyle or be a temporary patch for your life. You can't patch selfishness so you are only selfish fifty percent of the time! You can't put some of Jesus into one day of your week and be a real follower of Jesus. A radical change must occur in your life. As Jesus told Nicodemus, "You must be born again" (John 3:3).

Paul wrote: "Therefore, if anyone is in Christ, he is a new creation, old things have passed away, behold all things have become new" (2 Cor. 5:17). Jesus came to call sinners to repentance. When people come to

Jesus, He gives them a "do-over" in life. You can't be too sinful for Jesus to save, but you can think you are too good to need Jesus!

Jesus came to start a revolution. "Nor do they put new wine into old wineskins, or else the wineskins break, the wine is spilled, and the wineskins are ruined. But they put new wine into new wineskins, and both are preserved" (Matt. 9:17).

Wine was kept in leather bags made of sheepskin. Wine was the most common drink, but it was diluted with water, two parts water, to two parts wine. It was safer than much of their water supply. New leather would expand with the fermenting wine. The old leather was already stretched. New wine would make the old leather expand and burst.

The presence of Jesus signaled a new day. The teaching and healing ministry of Jesus was new and revolutionary, superseding the old religion of Judaism. Jesus was not pouring his new ministry into the old Judaism. The Jews had accumulated centuries of non-biblical traditions. Jesus was not defined or confined to the legalistic traditions of the Jews.

Jesus came to save. "But the days will come when the bridegroom will be taken away from them" (Matt. 9:15b). Jesus used the image of a wedding to portray the relationship between God and Israel. Examples from the Old Testament are Isaiah 54:1–8; Jeremiah 3:1–20, and Hosea 2:1–3:5. Jesus described Himself as the Messiah when He referred to Himself as the bridegroom. "Taken away" in verse 15 refers to Jesus' death on the cross to pay the penalty for our sins. Jesus' mission was to provide salvation for all those who would believe in Him as Lord and Savior. Jesus' sacrifice for sin ended the old animal sacrificial system. Why keep sacrificing animals when Jesus paid it all?

WHAT ARE THE TRUTHS FOR TODAY?

Paul wrote: "Rejoice in the Lord always" (Phil. 4:4). That rejoicing is made possible by the presence of the Bridegroom in our lives. The King of kings and the Lord of lords is here! The joy of the Lord should be the chief characteristic of a Christian.

Jesus came to do something new. He died on the cross for our sins. Jesus arose from the dead, conquering sin, death and hell and has prepared a place for us in heaven. He is coming again to receive believers unto Himself. Our mission is to live and talk about this good news so that others will enter into a personal relationship with Jesus.

Jesus did not come to patch up religion nor patch up our lives. Jesus came with a new covenant of grace written in His blood. Jesus offers everyone a radical change of life. "For the law was given by Moses, but grace and truth came by Jesus Christ" (John 1:17). Don't be satisfied with just trying to be a better person. Your life and your eternal destination can be changed by the saving power of Jesus. Commit your life to Jesus, the only One who can make you new!

Parable of the Sower
Matthew 13:1–9

¹"On the same day Jesus went out of the house and sat by the sea. ²And a great multitude gathered together to Him, so that He got into a boat and sat; and the whole multitude stood on the shore. ³Then He spoke many things to them in parables, saying: "Behold a sower went out to sow. ⁴And as he sowed, some fell by the wayside; and the birds came and devoured them. ⁵Some fell on stony places, where they did not have much earth; and they immediately sprang up because they had no depth of earth. ⁶But when the sun was up they were scorched, and because they had no roots they withered away. ⁷And some fell among thorns, and the thorns sprang up and choked them. ⁸But others fell on good ground and yielded a crop: some a hundredfold, some sixty, some thirty. ⁹He who has ears to hear, let him hear!"

One of the most familiar parables of Jesus is the parable of the sower. I believe the main aim of the parable was for people to examine their own lives and decide what type of "soil" they were. How receptive are you to a personal relationship with Jesus Christ? How receptive are you to living your life following the teachings and precepts of scripture? Is your life and your actions subject to the latest fads and concerns or teachings of society or the latest line on social media? Are you seeking to change lives for Christ and thus change society? Or have social morals of this present culture changed you? Paul wrote: "And do not be conformed to this world, but be transformed by the renewing of your mind, that you may prove what is that good and acceptable and perfect will of God" (Rom. 12:2).

CONTEXT

The passage begins: "On the same day ..." (Matt. 13:1). That was the day that the mother of Jesus and His half-brothers were looking for Jesus to persuade Him to come home and stop His public ministry (Matt. 12:46–50). That "day" also included Jesus healing people (Matt. 12:9) of various diseases (Matt. 12:15). Jesus explained the true nature of the Messiah (Matt. 12:17–21) and healed the blind and dumb demonic (Matt. 12:22–23). Jesus also charged the Pharisees with committing the unpardonable sin when they accused Jesus of casting out demons by the power of Satan (Matt. 12:24–32). The scribes and Pharisees wanted a sign for Jesus to prove who He was (Matt. 12:38–42).

In chapter 13, the various religious leaders had rejected Jesus, yet great multitudes followed Jesus. So Jesus entered the boat by the shore and the people (v. 2) gathered on the hillside, sloping to the shore of the lake. This made a perfect amphitheater. In verse 3, it is recorded that Jesus "spoke in parables." The word parable is made of two words. They mean "alongside of" and "to lay or place." Jesus took something people would understand and lay alongside the spiritual truth He was seeking to impart. So after a busy day of rejection, Jesus told them the parable of a farmer who went out to sow his field.

THE PARABLE

Although some of those in the crowd around Jesus were not farmers, they all would have been familiar with the process. Poor people would not have had a large field or oxen to pull a plow. They would have prepared a small plot of land by hand, using a primitive hand pushed plow or a sharp stick. Seed was sown by the method of broadcasting the seed by hand. Perhaps you have sown grass seed this way, by swinging a hand and some from side to side, tossing the seed on both sides and in front as you walk.

The seed fell on different types of ground:

In verse 4, some seed "fell by the wayside." Fields had narrow paths that separated one field from another, where the farmer and travelers might pass by. The path would be packed hard and the seeds were on top of the ground and the birds ate the seed.

In verse 5, some seed fell on "rocky places." Loose rocks would have been removed to help build a stone wall around the field. This was an underlying bed of rock just beneath the surface. There was no depth to the soil. The seeds would sprout but in the sun the plants would wither and die (Matt. 13:6).

In verse 7, some seed fell among "the thorns." The ground may have looked good and the thorny weeds may have been chopped down earlier. But the thorns grew and "choked" the plants and they died.

In verse 8, some seed fell on "good soil." There was no hard ground, no rocks, and no weeds. Later, there was a great crop: "hundredfold, sixty, and thirty." In New Testament times, an average harvest was less than eight to one. The crop results that Jesus declared were phenomenal.

THE EXPLANATION

In verses 18–23, Jesus began to explain to the twelve disciples and perhaps other listeners the meaning of the parable (Mark 4:10).

The hard-hearted hearer. The hard soil on the path represents the person who hears and yet rejects the truth that Jesus is the Son of God. These people are unconcerned about spiritual things. The Word of God that is "sown" does not penetrate that person's heart. So the Word is exposed to the enemy, "the wicked one" (Matt. 13:19), and he snatches it away. Any person's lack of repentance of their sin and faith in Jesus Christ leaves them vulnerable to attacks from Satan.

The shallow hearer. The second soil covers underlying rock and has no depth. This represents the person who hears the Word and receives it (Matt. 13:20). He may rejoice at the thought of eternal life. But his faith has no depth. That person did not accept the challenge of dying to himself, turning from his old life, and following the person and the teaching of Jesus. So at the first sign of tribulation or persecution, he fails (Matt. 13:21). We must enter into a life-changing, life-saving relationship with Jesus as Savior and Lord of our lives.

The word translated "stumbles" (Matt. 13:21) means "to cause to stumble or fall." The Greek word translated into English is the word "scandalize." The shallow hearer is offended, stumbles, and falls away.

The worldly hearer. The soil with the thorns that choke out the sprouts of the good seed represents the person who is attracted to the world and the things of the world. He is blinded to the gospel because the "cares" and "riches" of the world are more important than the Word of God (Matt. 13:22). The lust for things will crowd the Lord out of your life. John wrote: "Do not love the world or the things in the world. If anyone loves the world, the love of the Father is not in him. For all that is in the world — the lust of the flesh, the lust of the eyes, and the pride of life — is not of the Father but is of the world" (1 John 2:15–16).

The responsive hearer. The good soil is the person who hears the Word and understands it, because he accepts Jesus as his Lord and Savior. Jesus wanted to encourage the disciples with the truth that there is good soil. There are people who will respond in faith, and produce good works for the Lord's kingdom (Matt. 13:23).

Despite a day when Jesus faced rejection and hard-heartedness, there are people who will respond to Jesus in faith. True believers will bear fruits for the kingdom (Matt. 13:23b).

Meaning for Us Today

There are different responses to the gospel. Jesus did not tell this parable to discourage anyone. The point of the parable is that there is good soil. There are people who will respond in faith and bear much fruit for the kingdom of God. True believers are faithful, obedient followers of Jesus Christ whose lives will focus on serving Jesus.

We are all sowers today. In the parable, I believe Jesus is the sower. He came into the world to reveal His heavenly Father and provide salvation for all who truly believe in Him. But each of us must be a sower of the Word also. We do not sow any human organization, creed, opinion, idol or plan. We are to sow the Word of God, the gospel of our Lord Jesus Christ. Paul wrote: "… but we preach Christ crucified …" (1 Cor. 1:23). Believers in the Lord Jesus Christ have been entrusted with the Great Commission. Believers empowered by the Holy Spirit will be able to: "Go therefore and make disciples of all the nations, baptizing them in the name of the Father, the Son, and of the Holy Spirit, teaching them to observe all things that I have commanded you; and lo, I am with you always, even to the end of the age" (Matt. 28:19–20).

I would like to change the traditional name of this parable from "the parable of the sower" to the "parable of the abundant harvest." John wrote: "Then I looked, and I heard the voice of many angels around the throne, the living creatures, and the elders; and the number of them was ten thousand times ten thousand, and thousands of thousands, saying with a loud voice: "Worthy is the lamb who was slain to receive power and riches and wisdom and strength and honor and glory and blessing!" (Rev. 5:11–12)

Will you be in the great crowd gathered at the throne praising the Lord? Which type of hearer are you? Are you hard-hearted, or shallow, or worldly? Or are you a good listener who hears, understands, believes and follows Jesus?

PARABLE OF THE TWO SONS
MATTHEW 21:28-32

[28]"But what do you think? A man had two sons, and he came to the first and said, 'Son go, work today in my vineyard.' [29]He answered and said, 'I will not', but afterward he regretted it and went. [30]Then he came to the second and said likewise. And he answered and said, 'I go sir', but he did not go. [31]Which of the two did the will of his father? They said to Him, 'The first.' Jesus said to them, 'Assuredly, I say to you that tax collectors and harlots enter the kingdom of God before you. [32]For John came to you in the way of righteousness, and you did not believe him; but tax collectors and harlots believed him; and when you saw it, you did not afterward relent and believe him."

During Jesus' last week of earthly ministry, He was in Jerusalem. His parables focused on His acceptance or rejection by the people. Often people did not understand the truth and application of the parables, while being able to identify with the elements taken directly from common life factors. However, the priests and the Pharisees understood that Jesus was speaking about them (Matt. 21:45). The religious leaders were angered by Jesus' parables and in their pride and lust for power and wealth rejected Him. They refused to see the truth or seek forgiveness.

Jesus reminded His disciples of what Isaiah had predicted: "Keep on hearing, but do not understand; keep on seeing, but do not perceive.

Make the heart of this people dull" (Isaiah 6:9–10 and Matt. 13:14–15). The religious leaders fit the description of people with dull eyes, ears, and hearts. They needed to humble themselves before God and seek the truth.

CONTEXT

When Jesus rode into Jerusalem on a donkey, the people hailed Him as the Messiah. They cried out: "Hosanna to the Son of David" (Matt. 21:9). This aroused the religious leaders. And after Jesus cleansed the temple of those who were selling sacrificial animals and exchanging money, the chief priests and scribes were indignant (Matt. 21:15). The next day when Jesus came to the temple the chief priests and the elders confronted Jesus and demanded: "By what authority are you doing these things? And who gave you this authority?" Jesus knew their hearts and dumbfounded the religious leaders with a question about John's authority. They were not able to answer (Matt. 21:24–27). Then Jesus told the parable about a man with two sons.

THE PARABLE

Jesus told a simple and straightforward parable about a father with two sons. A father asked one son to go and work in his vineyard. The son responded "No!" He later regretted his decision and went to work in the vineyard. In the meantime, the father approached his second son and asked him to work in his vineyard. The second son told his father that he would go and work in the vineyard, but he did not.

Jesus then asked the hearers a question. Jesus wanted them to not only listen but to apply the parable to themselves: "Which of the two did the will of his father?" (Matt. 21:31). The people responded correctly: "The first." The son who actually worked in the vineyard was the obedient son.

THE MEANING OF THE PARABLE FOR US TODAY

Actions speak louder than words. The religious leaders were like the second son. They said everything in a proper, pious way, but were unfaithful in actual service! This was a word of judgment to those who then and now think they are saved by their rule keeping, their position, their heritage, their family or their good works. People are saved as they respond in obedience to Jesus Christ as their Lord and Savior. The faithfulness of the repentant sinner is far better than the disobedient, uncommitted, so-called believer who says all the right things and yet does not even attempt to live up to what they say. Don't be a great pretender of the faith. Be a great practitioner of the faith.

In Matthew 21:31–32, Jesus explained the reason for the judgment that would come upon the hypocritical religious leaders. Tax collectors and harlots were the two most despised categories of sinners in those days. But Jesus said they would enter the kingdom before the unfaithful and disobedient religious leaders, because the tax collectors and harlots had repented and believed when they heard the preaching of John the Baptist. They were disobedient at first, but turned and did the will of the Father, but the religious leaders said they were faithful, but they were disobedient and did not do the will of the Father.

There is a saying that being close doesn't count, except in horseshoes or hand grenades! Halfway or halfhearted doesn't count in faith either. You either work in your heavenly Father's vineyard or you don't. You either repent, believe, and obey Jesus or you don't. Your hope is all in Jesus or you have no hope at all. If you have no hope in Jesus this powerful word of judgment is for you!

SECTION III
PARABLES ON THE KINGDOM TO COME

Parable of the Wheat and the Tares
Matthew 13:24–30

²⁴"Another parable He put forth to them, saying: 'The kingdom of heaven is like a man who sowed good seed in his field, ²⁵but while men slept, his enemy came and sowed tares among the wheat and went his way. ²⁶But when the grain had sprouted and produced a crop, then the tares also appeared. ²⁷So the servants of the owner came and said to him, 'Sir, did you not sow good seed in your field? How then does it have tares?' ²⁸He said to them, 'An enemy has done this.' The servants said to him, 'Do you want us then to go and gather them up?' ²⁹But he said, 'No, lest while you gather up the tares you also uproot the wheat with them. ³⁰Let both grow together until the harvest, and at the time of harvest I will say to the reapers, 'First gather together the tares and bind them in bundles to burn them, but gather the wheat into my barn.'"

I read many years ago about a restaurant sign that declared that it offered "Complete Dinner Specials." However, for some reason, the "D" had dropped off the sign and the sign read "Complete Inner Specials." We need to be changed by the power of the Holy Spirit. Paul wrote: "Therefore, if anyone is in Christ, he is a new creation, old things have passed away, behold, all things have become new" (2 Cor. 5:17).

But how do we weed out all the evil thoughts, evil deeds, and disobedience to the known will of God for our lives? Matthew continued to report some of the parables of Jesus in chapter 13. The parable of the "wheat and the tares" should give us some answers to the question about what needs to be done and what will be done in our lives.

Context

In chapter 12, Matthew recorded that Jesus was rejected by the religious leaders (Matt. 12:24). Plots to destroy Jesus were being planned (Matt. 12:14). In spite of all the official opposition to Him, Jesus knew there would be an abundant harvest when He told the parable of the wheat and tares.

The Parable

The parable used the familiar scene of a farmer sowing seed in his field (v. 24). The emphasis of the parable of Jesus is not on what happened to the good seed, but what happened to the bad seed sown in the field by the enemy secretly (Matt. 13:25). "Tares" (v. 26) were a variety of darnel weed that closely resembles wheat. It is impossible to tell the difference between wheat and tares until the wheat ripens and the grain appears.

It was apparently a common practice in those days to destroy or damage an enemy's wheat crop by sowing tares in their field. It was so common a crime that the Romans had a law against it. Jesus knew His listeners would be familiar with this vengeful practice.

What was to be done? The servants knew good seed had been sown (v. 27). Obviously, an enemy had sown the tares (v. 28). The servants asked the owner if they should gather up the weeds (v. 28). The master responded "no," because they might also uproot the wheat (v. 29). They were instructed to allow them to grow together until the time of the harvest when they would be able to see the difference (v. 30). The tares were to be gathered and burned and the wheat would be gathered into the barn.

THE MEANING OF THE PARABLE

Later, when the multitude had left, the disciples of Jesus asked for an explanation of the parable (Matt. 13:36).

Jesus responded that the sower of the good seed is the Son of Man, Jesus Himself. The field is the world and the good seeds are "the sons of the kingdom," and the tares are "the sons of the wicked one" (Matt. 13:37–38). Jesus told them that the enemy who sowed tares is the devil, the harvest is the end of the age, and the reapers in the harvest are the angels (Matt. 13:39).

Jesus then gave a clear picture of judgment. Just as the tares are gathered and burned, so the judgment will come (Matt. 13:40). The Son of Man will send His angels and they will gather "those who practice lawlessness." They will be cast into the "furnace of fire," and there will be "wailing and gnashing of teeth" (Matt. 13:41–42). This is a clear picture of hell. Some might say that since Jesus is love, He would not send anyone to hell. Yet Jesus' words leave no doubt. Those who "practice lawlessness," whose lifestyle is in rebellion to the Lord's will and purpose, will be punished. The gracious promise of the Lord is also very clear. Those who are "righteous," right with the Lord by grace through faith, "will shine forth as the sun in the kingdom of their Father" (Matt. 13:43).

THE MEANING FOR US TODAY

There will be a final judgment. It is not our job to judge others. We can discern and realize by other people's lifestyles whether or not they are believers. In our judging we might damage the good we seek to do along with pointing out the bad. Judgment belongs to the Lord. Jesus is The Judge.

There will always be weeds. Satan is deceptive. He will be planting weeds that imitate the good crop. But when we experience the "weeds" in life we can ask for help.

When Jesus began this parable, He gave His listeners a "heads up." The parable was about the "kingdom of heaven" (v. 36). The disciples later asked for an explanation. Jesus wants us to pray, and study the Bible to seek answers to the deep questions of life. Jesus said: "He who has ears to hear, let him hear" (Matt. 13:43). Those who have ears listening to the voice of their Master Jesus, through faith, will hear and understand.

We must learn to wait on the Lord. The servants wanted to cut out the tares immediately. But the best method was to wait on the harvest. We may wonder why the Lord does not intervene in the midst of our problems and solve them now. However, waiting and trusting in the Lord helps us grow spiritually.

Judgment is coming. There is hell and there is heaven. In the meantime, we must work on the weeds in our own lives. We must evaluate our walk with the Lord Jesus. Are you following, and serving the Lord Jesus or seeking the things of this world? The Lord of the harvest knows who the pretenders are and those whose lifestyles are outside the laws of God.

Be alert, evil is at work. So many of our good intentions never come to fulfillment, because we fall asleep while evil is being sown (v. 25). Satan, apparently, doesn't take time off. He is at work to destroy you, or slow down your commitment to serve the Lord. Satan wants you to close your eyes to the mission field all around you. In Ephesians 6:10,11,13 Paul wrote: "Finally, my brethren, be strong in the Lord and in the power of His might. Put on the whole armor of God, that you may be able to stand against the wiles of the devil…Therefore take up the whole armor of God, that you may be able to withstand in the evil day, and having done all, to stand."

Parable of the Dragnet

Matthew 13:47–51

[47]"Again, the kingdom of heaven is like a dragnet that was cast into the sea and gathered some of every kind, [48]which, when it was full, they drew to shore; and they sat down and gathered the good into vessels, but threw the bad away. [49]So it will be at the end of the age. The angels will come forth, separate the wicked from among the just, [50]and cast them into the furnace of fire. There will be wailing and gnashing of teeth.' [51]Jesus said to them, 'Have you understood all these things?'"

Many years ago there was a very popular television drama about real police work entitled "Dragnet." As each episode unfolded, the police would gather the facts and the clues and gather up the criminals in their "dragnet."

Context

The word "dragnet" was a fishing term. It was very natural to use such a common and well-known term to explain a facet of the kingdom of heaven. In Palestine, there were two main ways of fishing. The first was to cast a net. This method could be used on the shoreline or from the bow of a boat. The net was attached to a large loop that was weighted. The fisherman would cast out the net, the loop would sink, and then the net would be drawn in by the fisherman. It was similar to a cowboy throwing his lasso to rope a steer.

The second method of fishing was using a dragnet. The net was a large square with chords at each corner and weights were attached on the bottom side. One side of the net would sink into the water and as the boat moved along, the net would catch anything in its path. The net would be drawn to shore and the fisherman would separate the catch. The good fish were kept, and everything else was thrown away.

THE MEANING OF THE PARABLE

Matthew closed out this chapter, which was full of Jesus' parables, with a parable of judgment. In Jesus' illustration, the kingdom of heaven is like a fisherman's dragnet. All types of fish were gathered. The fishermen then had to sort the good from the bad. The bad fish were cast out. So Jesus said, "at the end of the age" (v. 49), angels will come and "separate the wicked from the just" and the wicked will be "cast into the furnace of fire" (v. 50). A frequent phrase used in association with hell is that it will be a place of "wailing and gnashing of teeth" (v. 50). The vital question that Jesus asked His first hearers and us today is, "Do you understand?" (v. 51).

THE MEANING FOR US TODAY

The final judgment will come. In the judgment there will be a separation of good and evil. All people are not automatically going to heaven or hell. There will be a judgment. The basis of that judgment is whether or not you have trusted Jesus as your Lord and Savior and have sought to be obedient to Him.

The Church is caught in the dragnet. Today, the church includes all different types of people. It includes good and evil, saved and unsaved. But in the judgment, the Lord Jesus will sort all of this out. The righteous will be a part of God's eternal kingdom and non-believers will perish. The Bible declares: "It is the will of God that none should perish but that all would come in repentance" (2 Peter 3:9). God's desire is that all should come in repentance and believe in Jesus as their Lord and Savior. But if anyone refuses God's gracious offer of salvation through the shed blood of Jesus on the cross, there is no other way.

Jesus wept over Jerusalem and said, "O how often I would have gathered you under my wings as a hen does her chicks, but you would not" (Matt. 23:37). Judgment will begin with the church. "For the time has come for judgment to begin at the house of God" (1 Peter 4:17).

The wicked will be judged. The phrases "furnace of fire" and "wailing and gnashing of teeth" are graphic pictures of hell (v. 50). Fire is a frequent picture of hell. "Wailing" is a loud, uncontrollable weeping. This is not the sorrow of repentance, but a weeping over personal loss.

The real anguish is being completely separated from the presence of the Lord.

We can't imagine what it will be like to be "outside." No living person has yet experienced the horror of being completely severed from the presence of the Lord. The Lord has not removed His Holy Spirit from this world. The Lord is present in the lives of believers, and His blessings are seen in nature and all the bounty of the earth. But the unrepentant wicked will be removed from the presence of the Lord in the judgment. Those who trust in the Lord Jesus know the peace, joy and love of the Father.

All people must make a choice. Choose to enter the kingdom! Enter into the love and forgiveness of the Lord. Outside the kingdom there is nothing but hell. My prayer for you is that living for Jesus will be your daily goal.

Parable of the Wicked Vinedressers
Matthew 21:33–46

[33]"Hear another parable: There was a certain landowner who planted a vineyard and set a hedge around it, dug a winepress in it and built a tower. And he leased it to vinedressers and went into a far country. [34]Now when vintage-time drew near, he sent his servants to the vinedressers, that they might receive its fruit. [35]And the vinedressers took his servants, beat one, killed one, and stoned another. [36]Again he sent other servants more than the first, and they did likewise to them. [37]Then last of all he sent his son to them saying, 'They will respect my son.' [38]But when the vinedressers saw the son, they said among themselves, 'This is the heir. Come, let us kill him and seize his inheritance.' [39]So they took him and cast him out of the vineyard and killed him. [40]'Therefore when the owner of the vineyard comes, what will he do to those vinedressers?'

[41]They said to Him, 'He will destroy those wicked men miserably, and lease his vineyard to other vinedressers who will render to him the fruits in their seasons.' [42]Jesus said to them, 'Have you never read in the Scriptures: "The stone which the builders rejected has become the chief cornerstone. This was the Lord's doing, and it is marvelous in our eyes?"

[43]'Therefore I say to you, the kingdom of God will be taken from you and given to a nation bearing the fruits of it.

⁴⁴And whoever falls on this stone will be broken, but on whomever it falls it will grind him to powder.'
⁴⁵Now when the chief priests and Pharisees heard His parables, they perceived that he was speaking of them.
⁴⁶But when they sought to lay hands on Him, they feared the multitudes, because they took Him for a prophet."

In this parable Jesus continued to respond to His hostile rejection by the Jewish religious leaders. The religious leaders wanted a military Messiah that would defeat their earthly enemies and allow them to rule over their defeated foes. But when Jesus came, He came as the Prince of Peace. Jesus came as the suffering servant of Isaiah. The religious leaders were disappointed, and they realized that Jesus understood their corrupt character and their desire for wealth and power.

CONTEXT

The chief priests and elders demanded that Jesus tell them by what authority He had for His ministry (Matt. 21:23). The religious leaders were disturbed and angered that the crowd had proclaimed Jesus as the Messiah when He entered Jerusalem in what is called "the triumphal entry" (Matt. 21:9). After His entry, Jesus went to the temple and drove out all those who were buying and selling sacrificial animals and overturned the tables of the money changers (Matt. 21:12). The religious leaders were indignant (Matt. 21:15) and again questioned Jesus' authority.

THE PARABLE

Jesus told them a parable that really related the Lord's relationship with Israel. It is almost a summary statement of the Bible! It is the story of God's plan of salvation through history to that time.

It would have been easy for the hearers of the parable to understand the surface ideas of the parable. The hillsides of Palestine would have had many vineyards which were a great part of their economy. The owner of the land had made every preparation for the vineyard to be a success. He had a wall built to protect the harvest from wild animals or thieves. He dug down to bedrock to make a winepress. He then built a tower for a guard and a storage area. After making all careful preparations, the owner rented the property to some workers he thought were reliable, and then went on a journey (Matt. 21:33).

When harvest time came, the owner sent some servants to collect his share of the profits. But the wicked workers beat one, killed another, and stoned a third. Later, the owner sent a larger group of servants and they were also dealt with harshly by the vinedressers (Matt. 21:34–36).

Finally, the owner sent his son, thinking the workers would respect him. It seemed that at first, the workers were only going to keep all the profit from the vineyard, but now they saw the opportunity to take possession of the vineyard by killing the heir, the son (Matt. 21:37–39).

Jesus ended this dramatic parable in rabbinical fashion by asking his hearers: "What will the owner do to these vinedressers?" They responded: "He will destroy them and leave his vineyard to others who will be faithful in their duties" (Matt. 21:40–41). They did not realize they had pronounced their own guilty verdict.

THE MEANING OF THE PARABLE FOR US TODAY

First, some will reject Jesus. In a sarcastic question Jesus asked these authorities on the Scriptures: "Have you never read in the Scriptures …?" (Matt. 21:42). Jesus made the point of the parable by reminding them of the words of Psalm 118:22. Psalm 118 was one of the Hallel Psalms associated with Passover. The crowd had greeted Jesus by shouting that Jesus was the "Son of David" or the Messiah (Matt. 21:9), quoting from Psalm 118:26. Jesus pointed them to the verses concerning the stone rejected by the builders that became the chief cornerstone (Psalm 118:22–23). The cornerstone was the essential part of a building. Every other part of the building was determined by the proper placement of the cornerstone. Peter used this same passage later to proclaim that Jesus, who was crucified and resurrected, is the cornerstone and the One and only One who can provide salvation. (Acts 4:10–12).

Second, God has a plan. This parable declares that God created and provided everything necessary for us to have a relationship with Him. He continually sent prophets, leaders and teachers to the Jews to call them to repentance and faithfulness to the Lord. Time after time, the people rebelled and rejected the Lord. Finally, He sent His only begotten Son and they rejected and crucified Him.

God's plan also includes the truth that one day the owner will return. Jesus is coming back to claim His own and bring judgment upon those who have rejected Him (Matt. 21:41). Jesus made it clear that those who reject Him are like the wicked vinedressers who knew He was God's Son, but rejected Him anyway.

The word translated "nation" in verse 43 has the basic meaning of "people" (see Acts 8:9). The people who are to produce the fruit of the kingdom is the church. "... [A] chosen race, a royal priesthood, a holy nation, a people for God's own possession" (1 Peter 2:9).

The religious leaders in Jesus' day missed their opportunity to trust and honor the Son of God. How about you? Will you accept and obey Jesus as your Lord and Savior? Or will you miss your opportunity to have eternal life?

Parable of the Wedding Feast

Matthew 22:1–14

[1]"And Jesus answered and spoke to them again by parables and said: [2]'The kingdom of heaven is like a certain king who arranged a marriage for his son, [3]and sent out his servants to call those who were invited to the wedding; and they were not willing to come. [4]Again, he sent out other servants saying, "Tell those who are invited, 'See, I have prepared my dinner; my oxen and fatted cattle are killed, and all things are ready. Come to the wedding.' [5]But they made light of it and went their ways, one to his own farm, another to his business. [6]And the rest seized his servants, treated them spitefully, and killed them. [7]But when the king heard about it, he was furious. And he sent out his armies, destroyed those murderers, and burned up their city. [8]Then he said to his servants, 'The wedding is ready, but those who were invited were not worthy. [9]Therefore go into the highways, and as many as you find, invite to the wedding.' [10]So those servants went out into the highways and gathered together all whom they found, both bad and good. And the wedding hall was filled with guests. [11]"But when the king came in to see the guests, he saw a man there who did not have on a wedding garment. [12]So he said to him, 'Friend, how did you come in here without a wedding garment?' And he was speechless. [13]Then the king said to his servants,

*'Bind him hand and foot, take him away, and cast him
into outer darkness; there will be weeping and gnashing of
teeth.'* [14]*"For many are called, but few are chosen."*

CONTEXT

In verse 1, Matthew commented that Jesus "spoke to them again in
parables." The plural refers to the three parables: "The Parable of Two
Sons," "The Parable of the Wicked Vinedressers," and "The Parable of the
Wedding Feast."

The three parables grow in intensity. In the first parable, one son
refused to work in his father's vineyard, but regretted it and later did the
work. The second son agreed to work, but never did any work. The Jewish
leaders condemned themselves when they responded to Jesus that the
first son did the will of the Father.

In the Parable of the Wicked Vinedressers Jesus revealed God's plan
of salvation down through the centuries, culminating in the death of His
Son for the sins of the world. Because of the Jews' rejection of Jesus "the
kingdom would be taken from you and given to a nation bearing the fruits
of it" (Matt. 21:43).

These two parables are the immediate context for the third parable
about a king giving a great wedding feast for his son.

THE PARABLE

"The kingdom of heaven is like" (Matt. 22:2) means that this parable
contains truths about the kingdom of heaven. Marriages were arranged
in those days by the parents and involved a great feast (Rev. 19:6–10).
Depending upon the wealth of the family, the feast could last as much as
seven days.

Weddings followed a pattern. The couple first made a marriage
contract, which was the basis for the marriage (Mal. 2:14). Then about

a year later, the groom went to the bride's home where she was officially presented to the groom. Later, there was a nighttime procession to the groom's home for the wedding feast (Matt. 25:1–13). The wedding feast is often compared to God's kingdom (Matt. 8:11, 25:10; Isaiah 25:6; Luke 14:15–24; John 2:1–11; Rev. 19:7–9). It is obvious that in the parable that the king is God the Father and Jesus is the Son.

Two wedding invitations were sent out (Matt. 22:3). The first invitation was sent far enough ahead of time so that everyone could make plans to attend. Those who received the first invitation later received a second invitation when all was ready for the wedding. Since in God's timing all was ready, the invitation (Matt. 22:4) probably refers to the forerunner ministry of John the Baptist and to Jesus' ministry.

Some "made light of it" or did not care about the invitation and went about their regular routine (Matt. 22:5). They were so involved with the things of the world that they ignored the invitation of the king. This response may represent the attitude of the religious authorities to Jesus. The Jewish religious leaders were responsible for John the Baptist's death, the crucifixion of Jesus and the persecution of the early church (Matt. 22:6). The "burning of the city" could refer to the destruction of Jerusalem by Titus in AD 70.

Because the Jews, for the most part, rejected Jesus, the door was opened for the Gentiles to enter the kingdom. The invitation went out to all people (Matt. 22:8–10). Those in the highways (Gentiles) responded to the invitation.

One man who responded for the wedding from the "highway" did not properly prepare himself for the wedding. He was supposed to wear clean clothes, but he did not (Matt. 22:11–12). This was insulting to the king's gracious invitation. The garment may refer to the righteousness freely given to those who believe in Christ's atoning death on the cross. The man who refused to wear the correct garment was like the Jews who refused to obey the Lord. The man was then bound hand and foot and cast "into outer darkness" (Matt. 22:13), referring to the judgment of God.

Jesus closed the parable by saying: "For many are called, but few are chosen" (Matt. 22:14). All Israel had been invited, but only a few would believe in Jesus. The true Israel, the true people of God are those who believe and follow Jesus Christ as their Lord and Savior.

MEANING OF THE PARABLE

Jesus' call is a call to joy. The invitation of the Lord is a call to joy far greater than the joy of a wedding feast. Following Jesus is not the sadness of giving up earthly pleasures or worldly desires. Following Jesus is the joy of having Christ dwell in your heart now and an eternal home in heaven forever. You will miss eternal joy if you refuse the living invitation of the Lord.

Why would anyone refuse? Some refuse the invitation of Christ because they choose second best. In the parable one man went to his farm and another man went to his business instead of going to the wedding feast. These things are not immoral or evil in themselves. But in so doing, they missed the best that the Lord offered them. It is so easy to be involved in the day-by-day struggles of life, the pleasures of life, and the labor of life that we miss the call of God to eternal joy.

God's invitation to us comes because of His grace. It is a gift. In the parable those who responded to the invitation out in the highways had not earned nor deserved this favor from the king. Their invitation came from the kindness and generosity of the king.

The reason you and I receive an invitation to enter the kingdom is by the grace of God. Our salvation was made possible by the sacrificial death of Jesus on the cross. We are saved by grace. Our part is to accept God's gracious invitation by faith.

Parable of the Fig Tree

Matthew 24:32–35

32"Now learn this parable from the fig tree: When its branch has already become tender and puts forth leaves, you know that summer is near. 33So you also, when you see all these things, know that it is near — at the doors! 34Assuredly, I say to you, this generation will by no means pass away till all these things take place. 35Heaven and earth will pass away, but My words will by no means pass away."

Context

The last seven parables of the kingdom focus on the return of Jesus in His second coming and the final judgment. Jesus will come suddenly, at a time when people will not be expecting Him. The background of this parable is the response of Jesus to the question of the disciples: "Tell us when will all these things be? And what will be the sign of Your coming, and of the end of the age?" (Matt. 24:3).

Jesus' answer gave a broad sweep of history at the end of the age. Jesus spoke of "false messiahs" (Matt. 24:5), "wars and rumors of wars" (Matt. 24:6)," nation against nation" (Matt. 24:7), "famines, pestilences, and earthquakes" (Matt. 24:7); persecution (Matt. 24:9–10), deceiving false prophets (Matt. 24:11), "lawlessness will abound" (Matt. 24:12), a falling away (Matt.24:12); and the gospel preached in all the world (Matt. 24:14).

Jesus foretold a time of great tribulation (Matt. 24:21). At the close of the tribulation there will be violent cosmic disturbances (Matt. 24:29).

The true sign will be the Son of Man coming on the clouds of heaven with power and glory (Matt. 24:30; Dan. 7:13–14).

THE PARABLE

We can predict the coming of summer from certain signs. For example, we know summer is near when the branches of trees become tender and produce leaves (Matt. 24:32). Likewise, we know the end is coming when we see the signs Jesus described in Matthew 24.

"Generation" in verse 34 may mean "race." This could mean that Israel as a people will still exist and God will fulfill His promise to them. Also, this could mean a particular era or generation of people that will experience these end time events. That is, all these events will happen rapidly in one generation. "All these things" (Matt. 24:34), refers to the Antichrist, the tribulation, and the appearance of Jesus Christ in all His glory.

"… My words will by no means pass away" (Matt. 24:35). The words of Jesus are more true and everlasting than all the universe.

THE MEANING OF THE PARABLE

We must be alert to the signs of the times. We are to live in the eager anticipation of the return of Christ for His church. These signs that Jesus gave the disciples were reminders that He is coming. Jesus said: "… the end is not yet" (Matt. 24:6); and "All these things are the beginning of sorrows" (Matt. 24:8). The word "sorrows" literally means "birth pangs." The signs are meant to keep us on alert and to faithfully follow Jesus in our time of watching for His return.

The return of Jesus will be a specular second coming. When Jesus comes everyone will know: "For as the lightning comes from the east and flashes to the west, so also will the coming of the Son of Man be" (Matt. 24:27). "Then the sign of the Son of Man will appear in heaven, and then all the tribes of the earth will mourn, and they will see the Son of Man coming on the clouds of heaven with power and great glory" (Matt. 24:30). The time of Christ's return is known only to God (Matt. 24:36). Our task is not to speculate as to the exact timing of our Lord's return, but to be prepared and to be watching, and to be serving in His kingdom when Jesus returns.

Do not be discouraged. We should not be discouraged by the overwhelming wave of evil we are witnessing in our world today. Before the great tribulation I believe that Jesus will return for His true followers in what we call the rapture! Evil is abounding, but God is in control and He will bring history to His conclusion. That conclusion will involve both judgment and a new creation. Jesus said: "In My Father's house are many mansions, if it were not so, I would have told you. I go to prepare a place for you. And if I go and prepare a place for you, I will come again, and receive you to Myself; that where I am, there you may be also" (John 14:2–3).

The questions we must all answer for ourselves are:
- "Do we truly believe in Jesus Christ as our Lord and Savior?"
- "Are we watching and anticipating His return?"
- And when Jesus comes, "Will we be doing those things He has asked us to do for His kingdom?"

Parable of the Two Servants
Matthew 24:45–51

⁴⁵*"Who then is a faithful and wise servant, whom his master made ruler over his household, to give them food in due season? ⁴⁶Blessed is that servant whom his master, when he comes, will find so doing. ⁴⁷Assuredly, I say to you that he will make him ruler over all his goods. ⁴⁸but if that evil servant says in his heart, 'My master is delaying his coming,' ⁴⁹and begins to beat his fellow servants, and to eat and drink with the drunkards, ⁵⁰the master of that servant will come one day when he is not looking for him and at an hour that he is not aware of, ⁵¹and will cut him in two and appoint him his portion with the hypocrites. These shall be weeping and gnashing of teeth."*

CONTEXT

As with the parable of the fig tree, the context of the parable of two servants are the signs of the times and the end of the age. That would include the coming of false Christs, wars, famines, pestilences, earthquakes, persecution and the gospel preached in all the world. It would also include the great tribulation, the Antichrist, and the return of our Lord Jesus Christ. These things are recorded in Matthew 24:3–35.

The immediate context are the words of Jesus: "But if that day and hour no one knows, not even the angels of heaven, but My Father only" (Matt. 24:36). Jesus' coming will be unexpected. The faithful are to watch and be ready for the return of Jesus Christ.

THE PARABLE

There are two servants in this parable of Jesus. They are examples of the two attitudes that people have about the second coming of Jesus.

The faithful and wise servant was put in charge of his master's household. He left this servant ruler over all he had and apparently went on a journey (Matt. 24:45). This servant was truly blessed when his master returned and found his servant faithfully discharging his duties (Matt. 24:46). As a reward for his faithful service, even in the absence of his master, the faithful servant was made the ruler over all the master's goods (Matt. 24:48). The other servant began to reason that the master was not coming soon (Matt. 24:48). So he began to treat his fellow servants cruelly. He also began to eat and drink with the drunkards (Matt. 24:49). The master returned expectantly and punished that wicked servant. "Cut in two" was a form of punishment in the ancient world. This would have been easily understood by those hearing this parable. The evil servant would be condemned with other hypocrites in the place where there is "weeping and gnashing of teeth" (Matt. 24:50–51). "Weeping and gnashing of teeth" is a description of the agony of hell, being separated from God and all that is good.

THE MEANING OF THE PARABLE

The faithful are watchful. A thief does not announce when he is coming to burglarize your house. He comes when he thinks he has the element of surprise or when your house is not protected (Matt. 24:43). But a Christian is guarding or watching for a surprise raid or attack. Christians are eagerly watching for the return of their Savior with joy.

Judgment will come. The evil servant in the parable thought it would be a very long time before his master returned. Judgment so long postponed became judgment forgotten in his mind. He was cruel to the other servants and began to live the party life of the rich. Does that remind you of the Washington swamp? However, his master did return and justice was swift and final. The evil servant was cast out and there was "weeping and gnashing of teeth." That is a description of eternal hell and punishment.

Faithfulness will be rewarded. The faithful servant, when his master returned he was made "ruler over all his goods" (Matt. 24:47).

When Jesus comes will he find you doing what He had asked you to do? The reward for faithful Christians is to live for all eternity in the presence of our Lord and Savior Jesus Christ.

Parable of the Wise and Foolish Virgins
Matthew 25:1–13

[1]"Then the kingdom of heaven shall be likened to ten virgins who took their lamps and went out to meet the bridegroom. [2]Now five of them were wise, and five were foolish. [3]Those who were foolish took their lamps and took no oil with them, [4]but the wise took oil in their vessels with their lamps. [5]But while the bridegroom was delayed, they all slumbered and slept. [6]And at midnight a cry was heard: 'Behold the bridegroom is coming; go out to meet him!' [7]Then all those virgins arose and trimmed their lamps. [8]And the foolish said to the wise, 'Give us some of your oil, for our lamps are going out.' [9]But the wise answered saying, 'No, lest there should not be enough for us and you; but go rather to those who sell, and buy for yourselves.' [10]And while they went to buy, the bridegroom came, and those who were ready went in with him to the wedding; and the door was shut. [11]Afterward the other virgins came also, saying, 'Lord, Lord, open to us!' [12]But he answered and said, 'Assuredly, I say to you, I do not know you.' [13]Watch therefore, for you know neither the day nor the hour in which the Son of Man is coming."

CONTEXT

The theme of these last three parables of Jesus, recorded in Matthew's gospel, is the unexpected return of Jesus Christ. The signs of the last times were given by Jesus. The warning of these parables is that people should be prepared by faithfully serving Jesus. Their preparation is faithful service to what Jesus has asked us to do. Then we are to live believing in His return and watching with anticipation and joy for His coming.

THE PARABLE

A wedding was the most joyous event in Jewish life. Their wedding customs and procedures may seem strange to us; they are so different. There was a wedding "parade." The whole village would accompany the couple to their new home, winding its way throughout the village.

When a couple married, they went home, instead of going away somewhere on a honeymoon. They were treated like royalty, and the wedding feast could last a week if they could afford it.

The virgins in the parable were young, unmarried women who would be like bridesmaids today. They would keep the bride company while they were waiting for the groom to come. Part of the fun was for the groom to come unexpectedly sometimes in the middle of the night. No one knew when the groom would arrive. However, right before the bridegroom would come, he would send a man through the streets shouting: "Behold! The bridegroom is coming!" Everyone had to be ready at any time to go into the street and meet the bridegroom. No one was allowed to be on the streets at night without a lamp. There were, of course, not any street lights. Once everyone arrived, the door was shut and no one else was allowed to enter. That is the background of this parable of Jesus.

In the parable, five virgins were wise and five were foolish. Personal lamps were usually small lamps made of clay. There was a hole in the top to pour in oil and a spout-like feature for a small cloth wick to protrude on one side. The wick was lighted and would provide some light to help a person walk through the streets after dark. The five foolish virgins did not bring any extra oil to replenish their small lamps. They arrived late at the home for the wedding feast and were denied entry.

THE MEANING OF THE PARABLE

Preparation is key. We must be prepared for the return of Christ. The only way to be prepared is to be saved by grace through faith in Jesus as your personal Lord and Savior. You can't wait until the last minute. You don't know when your death will occur or when Christ will return. So you don't know when the last minute will be!

It is too late if you wait until the morning of your final exams to study. Perhaps you have heard of death-bed confessions of faith. That has happened. But if you wait all your life to commit your heart to Jesus, you may not be alert or aware when suddenly your life is over. If you haven't done so, trust Jesus now. Believe that Jesus is the Son of God, who came to this earth and died on a cross to pay the penalty for your sin and rose again from the dead that He may give to all who believe in Him eternal life.

Some things can't be borrowed. We may borrow some items from a friend to use temporarily. But you cannot borrow godly character from anyone. You cannot borrow from your parents or anyone else their gift of eternal life. You must do this for yourself.

The foolish virgins in this parable could not borrow oil when they needed it. You cannot borrow a personal relationship with Jesus either. You will not be ready when Jesus comes if you are depending on the spiritual lives of other church members or family or friends. We cannot borrow spiritual character, we must live it, experience it, and practice it for ourselves.

We will have no spiritual light to guide us when we discover that our lamps are empty. Is your life empty or have you been filled with the Holy Spirit? Paul wrote: "… Christ in you, the hope of glory" (Col. 1:27).

Commit your heart and life to Jesus now. Be ready when Jesus Christ comes for you or comes for His church.

When I was a child we played a game called "hide and seek." One person was "it" and he was to search and find all the other children who were hiding. If you could come to the "home base" while the seeker was away, you were "home free." Before the seeker started his search, he would shout, "Ready or not, here I come!"

Ready or not, Jesus is coming. The only way you will be home free is to commit your life to Jesus Christ as your Lord and Savior now.

Parable of the Talents
Matthew 25:14-30

¹⁴"For the kingdom of heaven is like a man traveling to a far country, who called his own servants and delivered his goods to them.

¹⁵"And to one he gave five talents, to another two, and to another one, to each according to his own ability; and immediately he went on a journey.

¹⁶"Then he who had received the five talents went and traded with them, and made another five talents.

¹⁷"And likewise he who had received two gained two more also

¹⁸"But he who had received one went and dug in the ground, and hid his lord's money.

¹⁹"After a long time the lord of those servants came and settled accounts with them.

²⁰"So he who had received five talents came and brought five other talents, saying, 'Lord, you delivered to me five talents, look, I have gained five more talents besides them.

²¹"His lord said to him, 'Well done, good and faithful servant; you were faithful over a few things, I will make you ruler over many things. Enter into the joy of your lord.'

²²"He also who had received two talents came and said, 'Lord, you delivered to me two talents; look, I have gained two more talents besides them,'

[23]"His lord said to him, 'Well done, good and faithful servant; you have been faithful over a few things, I will make you ruler over many things. Enter into the joy of your lord.'

[24]"Then he who had received the one talent came and said, 'Lord, I knew you to be a hard man, reaping where you have not sown, and gathering where you have not scattered seed.

[25]"And I was afraid, and went and hid your talent in the ground. Look, there you have what is yours;

[26]"But his lord answered and said to him, 'You wicked and lazy servant, you knew that I reap where I have not sown, and gather where I have not scattered seed.'

[27]"Therefore, you ought to have deposited my money with the bankers, and at my coming I would have received back my own with interest.

[28]"Therefore take the talent from him, and give it to him who has ten talents.

[29]"For everyone who has, more will be given, and he will have abundance; but from him who does not have, even what he has will be taken away.

[30]"And cast the unprofitable servant into the outer darkness. There will be weeping and gnashing of teeth."

TALENT

It is first of all important to understand what a "talent" was in Jesus' day. A "talent" was a weight of coins, usually silver. A talent was worth about six thousand denarii. One denarius was a day's wage for an ordinary working man. One talent would represent the earnings of an ordinary worker for about eighteen years. Five talents would equal the wages for a worker equal to ninety years earnings. Two talents would represent thirty-six years of earnings. How much do you earn in a year? Do the math. These talents represent huge amounts of money that was entrusted to these servants.

CONTEXT

Although the parable begins, "For the kingdom of heaven is like ...," it is not just about how to conduct yourself as members of God's kingdom here on earth. Beginning in chapter 24, Matthew's sequence of Jesus' teachings is about the signs of the times, the end of the age and the return of Christ. "For as the lightning comes from the east and flashes to the west, so also will the coming of the Son of Man be" (Matt. 24:27). Matthew wrote about the coming of the Son of Man (Matt. 24:29–31) in the parable of the fig tree (Matt. 24:32–35), which speaks of Christ's return. But no one knows the day or hour of Christ's coming (Matt. 24 :36–44). The idea of the Master returning at His appointed time is taught in the parable of the faithful servant and the evil servant (Matt. 24:45–51); the parable of the wise and foolish virgins (Matt. 25:1–13); and the parable of the talents in Matthew 25:14–30.

The teaching of Jesus about His return and the final judgment immediately follows in Matthew 25:31–46. "When the Son of Man comes in His glory, and all the holy angels with Him, then He will sit on the throne of His glory. All the nations will be gathered before Him, and He will separate them from one another, as a shepherd divides his sheep from the goats" (Matt. 25:31–32).

THE PARABLE

Jesus took an earthly illustration and gave it a heavenly meaning. The parable is about "a man traveling to a far country" (Matt. 25:14). It was not uncommon in Jesus' day for a Jewish businessman to travel to other countries on business or trading enterprises. What may be unusual is that while he was gone he turned over the management of "his goods" to three servants. The servants were entrusted with great responsibilities and would be expected to give an account when the master returned. The servants apparently did not know when the master would return, but it was a "long time" (Matt. 25:19).

When the master returned the accounting was made. The first two servants had been "good and faithful" (Matt. 25:21–23). They both heard their master say "Well done," and they were given even greater responsibilities. They were invited to "enter into the joy of their lord."

But one servant with the one talent was afraid and buried the money entrusted to him in the ground. His master was not pleased and called him a "wicked and lazy servant" (Matt. 25:26). This "unprofitable servant" (Matt. 25:30) was cast into "outer darkness" where there is "weeping and gnashing of teeth" (Matt. 25:30). This is a common description of eternal separation from the Lord in hell.

It is obvious that the master in the parable is Jesus. Before Jesus ascended into heaven, He had left His followers in charge of the work of His earthly kingdom. Jesus gave them their marching orders: "All authority has been given Me in heaven and on earth. Go therefore and make disciples of all the nations, baptizing them in the name of the Father and of the Son and of the Holy Spirit, teaching them to observe all things that I have commanded you; and lo, I am with you always, even to the end of the age" (Matt. 28:18–20).

Jesus has given each of His followers not only material resources, but time, energy, abilities and spiritual gifts. One day Jesus will return and there will be a judgment. There will be an accounting, a final audit for how we have handled our responsibilities. Will you hear, "Well done, good and faithful servant"? Or will you hear, "Cast the unprofitable servant into outer darkness"? We were not saved to just sit in a pew, we were saved to serve. Works do not save, but those who are saved work. The Lord has entrusted to believers the work of the kingdom. Jesus is present with His followers to empower them to do the work He has called them to do. Paul wrote: "Christ in you, the hope of glory" (Col. 1:27).

TRUTHS FOR TODAY

This parable is about being trustworthy and hard-working in the management of money. This parable is not about the wise use of your time, service, ability, or gifts. Although this parable of Jesus could be applied to these areas, the question the parable raises is: "How do you handle your money?" I heard a preacher say many years ago, "show me your checkbook and I will know your priorities." I suppose now we might say, "show me your credit card statement and I will know your priorities." There is another old saying, "Put your money where your mouth is." If you say you love the Lord, is it reflected in the way you spend your money?

The first two servants received the same reward, even though they had been given different amounts of money. Both servants heard their master say, "Well done, good and faithful servant; you have been faithful over a few things, I will make you ruler over many things. Enter into the joy of your lord" (Matt. 25:21, 23). The Lord rewards His faithful followers. There are three rewards mentioned in the parable: (1) The faithful will hear the Lord say "Well done!" (2) The two servants were given greater responsibilities. (3) And the greatest reward is the invitation to enter into the joy of the Lord!

However, the wicked servant was lazy and unfaithful. Although he knew his master was capable of "reaping where you had not sown" and "gathering where you have not scattered seed" (Matt. 25:24), he was afraid and buried his money in the ground. He must have felt that the money was safe in the ground. The servant was able to return the money that the master had given him (Matt. 25:25). But his master responded that the servant was wicked and lazy (Matt. 25:26) and he should have at least put the money with bankers and earned some interest (Matt. 25:27). This unprofitable servant was cast into "outer darkness" (Matt. 25:30).

When Jesus comes again there will be a great judgment. All will have to answer for what they have done that is sinful and what they have failed to do with the resources the Lord has given us.

The parable teaches that a person must use what the Lord has given to them, for the glory of the Lord. If not, they will be judged as wicked and lazy and unprofitable in the judgment.

The focus of the parable is on the use of money, but the same judgment will apply as to how we use our spiritual gifts and abilities that the Lord has given us. We will be held accountable for how we use what we have been given by the Lord for His honor and glory.

Conclusion

When John the Baptist, the forerunner of Jesus, began his public ministry to prepare the way for the coming Messiah, his message was: "Repent, for the kingdom of heaven is at hand!" (Matt. 3:2). Later when Jesus began His public ministry the summary headline of His message was: "Repent, for the kingdom of heaven is at hand" (Matt. 4:17).

The heart of the message of Jesus was an invitation to enter the kingdom of heaven. Jesus made possible a person's entrance to the kingdom when He shed His blood on the cross to pay the penalty for our sin. We deserve to die for our sin, but Jesus took our place and paid the price for our sin. When we respond in faith to the gracious invitation of Jesus, we can enter the kingdom.

The kingdom was present in the world because Jesus was present in the world. "But Jesus said, "Let the little children come to Me, and do not forbid them; for of such is the kingdom of heaven" (Matt. 19:14). Wherever Jesus went, the kingdom was present. People could enter the kingdom, the rule and reign of the Lord Almighty in their hearts, when they responded to the invitation of Jesus.

The kingdom is also future. The writer of Hebrews reasoned that: "There remains therefore a rest for the people of God" (Heb. 4:9). The kingdom is a place where believers will be in the presence of the Lord. Jesus said: "In My Father's house are many mansions, if it were not so, I would have told you. I go to prepare a place for you. And if I go and prepare a place for you, I will come again and receive you to Myself; that where I am, there you may be also" (John 14:2–3).

The kingdom is here and now as the Holy Spirit dwells in the lives of believers. Paul wrote: "Now He who has prepared us for this very thing is God, who also has given us the Spirit as a guarantee" (2 Cor. 5:5).

The parables of Jesus were common everyday illustrations used to explain the kingdom, so that people who responded in faith to Jesus could understand. The parables are vital for us to understand the message of Jesus. In His own words Jesus used earthly events or examples from common life to help people comprehend the truth of the kingdom. This would help people know how to enter the kingdom and find the joy of the Lord in His presence forever.

It is my prayer that, in studying the parables of Jesus about His kingdom, you will have a greater understanding of His message. And that if you grow in your understanding, you will make a faith commitment to follow Jesus. I pray you will grasp the glory that awaits all believers who will be gathered around God's throne in His heavenly kingdom.

Appendix

Our granddaughter, Grace Dender, is a student at the New Orleans Baptist Theological Seminary. After I had finished this book , Grace wrote a school paper about one of the parables. I wanted to include her excellent paper in this appendix.

WORKSHEET #3

A Paper
Submitted to Dr. Charlie Ray III
of the
New Orleans Baptist Theological Seminary
In Partial Fulfillment
of the Requirements for the Course
Interpreting the New Testament 1: NTEN5351
in Biblical Studies

Grace E. Dender
BSN, Belmont University, 2021

Literary Context

Introduction

By studying the literary context of the parable of the wedding banquet found in Matthew 22:1–14, the reader is able to attain valuable insights into the intended audience and meaning of the passage. Though chapter 20 provides fundamental knowledge to the setting, the sections of Matthew most relevant to the literary context were Matthew chapters 21–23. Each chapter points to their interconnectedness and contributes to the overarching lesson by containing key words and themes that are repeated throughout. The author of Matthew compiled a group of narratives and parables to go along with the parable of the wedding banquet. Through examining the literary context of the passage, the text can be better understood and emphasized.

Setting

There are several key details important to the setting of the parable. The opening narrative of this set of passages is significant because Jesus is entering Jerusalem and His arrival to the city means that His death is imminent (Matt. 20:18–19)[1]. Jesus had already indicated that the chief priests and scribes would play a role in His condemnation and death (20:18) which is brought even further into focus through the series of parables introduced in this portion of the Gospel. What Jesus' arrival to

---

1 Unless otherwise noted, all Scripture references will be found from the CSB.

Jerusalem meant provides information foundational to fully understanding the driving force behind the telling of the parable of the wedding banquet.

AUDIENCE

It is essential to identify the parable's intended audience which can be found in Matthew 21. The religious leaders question Jesus and His authority when they saw Him teaching (21:23). Jesus responds with a question that they are unable to answer and follows their silence with three parables. There can be no mistake for the object of the parable's lesson: the religious leaders "knew He was speaking about them" (21:45). The parable was "directed specifically at those leaders and all unbelieving Israel whom they represented."[2]

MOTIFS

Recurring words and themes located within the selected passages serve to reveal the heart of the issue. Key words include the following: "fruit," "son," "servant," and "the kingdom." The themes of rejection, murder, and judgment are also repeated. Many of the words and concepts overlap with one another. The identification of repeated ideas helps to bring into focus the highlighted motifs surrounding the parable of the wedding banquet which convey the main point.

Within the particular group of narratives and parables, the first introduction to the concept of fruit is observed in the account of the barren fig tree (Matt. 21:18–19). In the narrative, Jesus comes upon a fig tree but finds it to be fruitless. In response, Jesus curses the fig tree which immediately withers. The judgment on the barren tree is not isolated. In fact, Jesus introduces parables in which the judgment of not producing fruit is unmistakable:

2 John MacArthur, *Matthew 16–23 MacArthur New Testament Commentary*, The MacArthur New Testament Commentary (Chicago: Moody Publishers, 1988), 179.

It results in the kingdom being taken away (21:43). There is also a parallel found previously in the Gospel which offers further understanding. When John the Baptist sees the Pharisees and Sadducees, he calls them a brood of vipers and says "Who warned you to flee from the coming wrath? Therefore, produce fruit consistent with repentance" (Matt. 3:8). Entry into the kingdom was directly related to repentance and the fruit produced as a result. For those who did not heed the command, judgment was inevitable. Though the word "fruit" is not found in the parable of the wedding banquet, the theme is still present. The wedding garment, which will be further explained within its historical cultural context, "stands for the lack of doing good. In the course of the narrative theology of the parable trilogy, the motif of doing the will of the Father (Matt. 21:31) and producing fruit (21:41, 43) is here carried further."[3] Bearing fruit or the lack thereof, was frequently referenced in the three chapters in both account and parables.

Another reiterated topic is sonship. The first mention of sonship is in response to Jesus. The crowd identifies Jesus as "the Son of David" (Matt. 21:9, 15) when He first enters the city. Matthew alludes to the truth of the statement by indicating that Jesus was in fact the fulfillment of the Old Testament prophecies (21:4–5, 9). Jesus also makes a clear connection by referring to Himself as the fulfillment of Psalm 118:22–23 when the people's response is brought into question by the religious leaders (Matt. 21:42). Additionally, the first parable introduced contains two sons: one who does the will of the father and the one who does not (21:28–30). In the second parable, the landowner sends his son to harvest the fruit but is disrespected and killed by the tenant farmers (21:39). The parable of the wedding banquet also includes the son whose wedding is the cause of celebration (22:2). Because of its presence in the narrative and parables, sonship could be presented as another motif.

---

3 MacArthur, 329.

The theme of rejection is also seen through the responses of the religious leaders and the characters in the parables. The disgruntled chief priests and elders refused to accept Jesus' authority as the Son of God, questioning Him (Matt. 21:23). Jesus responds with a parable. Through His story of the two sons, Jesus indicates that the son who was rebellious at first but later changed his mind, did the will of the father. On the other hand, the second son obeyed in speech but not in action and therefore did not do the father's will. Jesus follows the parable with a clear and pointing explanation. Jesus explicitly tells the chief priest and the elders that those they considered "less-than" such as tax collectors and prostitutes were entering the kingdom of heaven before them. These individuals believed while the leaders did not (21:28–32). In the second parable, the tenant farmers reject the servants sent to the harvest by beating or killing them (21:35–36). Furthermore, they rejected the son when he was sent to the vineyard and killed him too (21:39). Jesus once again provides the connection by telling the religious leaders that because of their rejection of Jesus (21:42), the kingdom of God would be taken away and given to those who produced fruit (21:43). Rejection also makes an appearance in the wedding banquet: the servants are sent to summon the invited guests but were ignored, seized, mistreated, and killed (22:5). The invitation itself was despised. Rejection is one of the major concerns and is extensively addressed within the series of passages.

CONCLUSION

After gathering information regarding the setting, audience, as well as the common and repetitive themes surrounding the passage, the parable's main idea of judgment comes into full view. The religious leaders had not only responded in indignance (21:14–15), refusal to believe (21:32) and rejection of the Son (21:42) but they plotted to kill Jesus (22:15). They proved themselves to be the subject of the parables. The main idea of the series of passages can be concluded in Matthew 23, which speaks to religious hypocrisy and the attached judgment. Sometimes the meanings of the parables were not entirely clear to His audience, but the point was not to be missed. The author of the Gospel was primarily focused on religious hypocrisy, what it looked like, and the consequences through the organization of the parables and narratives. Jesus specifically calls the religious leaders out and pronounces judgment upon those who refused to believe, did not repent, and did not produce fruit consistent with these actions. The invitation to enter the Kingdom of God had been sent out but had repeatedly been rejected invoking judgment if repentance did not take place.

HISTORICAL CULTURAL CONTEXT

INTRODUCTION

With the focus on the religious leaders and their representation of Israel, an understanding of the Jewish historical cultural context is beneficial. I identified a few main points of focus for the parable of the wedding banquet including customs of the wedding banquet, invitations, the honor of a king, and Old Testament implications. In studying the historical and cultural context, one is able to see through the lenses of Jesus' audience and to recognize the thoughts and responses that would have been invoked upon hearing the message.

CUSTOMS AND INVITATIONS

An invitation to a wedding feast meant to participate in a great celebration. Wedding festivities lasted at least seven days according to Jewish tradition.[4] For this reason, it was a valuable time commitment to

---

4 Craig S. Keener, *IVP Bible Background Commentary: New Testament.* 2nd ed., IVP Bible Background Commentary (Downers Grove: IVP Academic, 2014), 92.

come to a wedding[5], but to not attend would have meant great shame for both the host and the guest[6]. Weddings were of great importance[7] and many people would be invited, especially in the case of wealthy families.[8] The opportunity to attend such a joyous occasion would be considered "the highlight of all social life"[9] and would not be taken lightly.

During the time of Jesus, it was customary to receive two wedding invitations[10]. The initial invitation was sent prior to the readiness of preparations. By sending the invitation in advance, time would be allowed for the guests to make the appropriate arrangements needed to attend.[11] The invitation would have required a response, and though it was possible to decline such an invitation, to do so was a great insult to the host.[12] The second invitation was sent to the guests expected to attend once the preparations were ready (22:4). In the parable of the wedding feast, the words "to summon those invited" (22:3) signifies that the guests had already received their initial invitation and given their confirmation to attend.[13] When the time of the wedding banquet came, however, the guests in the parable scorned their host by refusing to come. It would have been a great offense to decline the first invitation, but even more so to repeal one's response. In fact, to "refuse after having agreed to come would be no accident, but a deliberately treasonous insult."[14] To receive two invitations to a wedding

5 Ibid.

6 Alan R. Culpepper, *Matthew: A Commentary*. 1st ed., New Testament Library (Louisville: Westminster John Knox Press, 2021), 322.

7 Craig A. Evans and Stanley E. Porter, *Dictionary of New Testament Background,* (Downers Grove: IVP Academic, 2000), 872.

8 Ibid.

9 MacArthur, 180.

10 Keener, 92.

11 Culpepper, 322.

12 Keener, 92.

13 Ibid.

14 Ibid.

feast meant that there had been time to plan and prepare for attendance and the insult of the guests' refusal in the parable is heightened.

THE KING

Of greater significance is the fact that the invitation was extended by the king. Jesus' audience would have easily understood that it was a great honor and privilege to attend the wedding of the king's son.[15] To refuse such a request made by the king was also an offense that could bear dire consequences.[16] A king had authority by functioning as both military leader and supreme judge[17] and was not to be ignored. In the parable, some of the guests do exactly this and pay no mind to the king's persistent request for their attendance (22:5). The listeners would have likely been shocked by the act of defiance and intentional dishonoring of the king. The audience would have been even more surprised by the actions that follow. Some of the other invited guests seize the king's servants, mistreat, and kill them (22:5). "Contempt for the king's slaves demonstrated contempt for the king himself, and in mistreating and killing his slaves they committed a flagrant act of rebellion."[18] This action invokes an appropriate response by the king: he is furious and sends his troops to execute the rebels and burn their city (22:7).

WEDDING ATTIRE

In the parable, the king notices that one of his guests is not wearing the appropriate clothing (22:11). Similar to today, wedding guests during Jesus' day would wear finer clothing than everyday wear.[19] Sometimes such

---

15 MacArthur, 180.

16 Ibid.

17 Chad Brand, Charles Draper, and Archie England, *Holman Illustrated Bible Dictionary* (Nashville: Holman Bible Publishers, 2003), 988.

18 MacArthur, 181.

19 Brand, Draper, and England, 1082.

clothing would even be "provided by wealthy families."[20] For this reason, it would have been likely that someone who was invited to a royal wedding would have been provided the necessary attire for the special occasion and would not have been responsible for it themselves.[21] The king in Jesus' parable seems to follow this tradition because "the fact that all of the dinner guests except that one man dressed in wedding clothes indicates that the king had made provisions for such clothes."[22] By equipping the guests with the needed garments, there was no excuse. The man in the parable was accountable for his actions.[23] The guest would have been deliberately refusing to wear what had been offered[24] and thereby mocking the host.

OLD TESTAMENT IMPLICATIONS

Since Jesus' target audience were the religious leaders, they had extensively studied the Old Testament Scriptures. They would have been familiar with passages in Isaiah and perhaps Jesus was drawing to mind two specific texts that make reference to a great banquet. One text highlights Israel's future glory (Isa. 54) and the other contained the day of salvation and judgment (Isa. 25). Both make reference to a great feast hosted by God on that day. "When the prophets of Israel envision a new age of peace and righteousness, they picture Yahweh hosting a lavish banquet."[25] Isaiah also "used marriage imagery to express God's love for Israel and a parable about a king, the king's son, and a wedding feast would resonate with biblical images and metaphors."[26] With their Scriptural knowledge and

---

20 Ibid.
21 John Phillips, *Exploring the Gospel of Matthew,* The John Phillips Commentary Series (Grand Rapids: Kregel Publications, 1999), 418.
22 MacArthur, 183.
23 Ibid.
24 Phillips, 418
25 Philip J. King and Lawrence E. Stager. *Life In Biblical Israel* (Louisville: John Knox Press, 2001), 354.
26 Culpepper, 323.

Jesus' explicit statement that he was sharing a parable about the kingdom (Matt. 22:2), the religious leaders could not miss the message.

Furthermore, the punishment of being cast out into the "outer darkness" (22:13) had significant meaning. "Darkness was thought of as a curse and frequently associated with supernatural events involving the judgment of God. Darkness also forms part of God's punishment on the disobedient. Darkness often had an ethical sense and symbolizes ignorance, especially of God and of God's ways.."[27] The Scripture speaks to it in Isaiah 8:22 and 9:2. The punishment was so great and the "gnashing of teeth displays the raging despair of those excluded from Christ's kingdom."[28] There would have been a stark contrast to the brightly lit banquet and the darkness of night, but to be thrown out of the celebration and cast into the darkness had a deeper implication of God's judgment.

CONCLUSION

The understanding of the parable of the wedding banquet can be aided through the study of the literary, historical, and cultural context. By organizing the narratives and parables that relate to the great wedding feast, the author of Mark emphasized the lesson to be learned by the Gospel's reader. Religious hypocrisy would not be left unpunished. Entrance to the Kingdom of God was dependent on the belief that Jesus was the Son of God, repentance, and actions reflecting a changed heart. Jesus provides a story that His audience could easily relate to and though His message is timeless, knowledge of the historical cultural context allows the reader to fully grasp what the audience understood in this chapter of Matthew.

---

27 Brand, Draper, and England, 390.
28 Ibid., 1559.

SELECTED BIBLIOGRAPHY

Brand, Chad., Charles Draper, and Archie England. *Holman Illustrated Bible Dictionary*. Nashville: Holman Bible Publishers, 2003.

Culpepper, Alan R. *Matthew: A Commentary*, 1st ed. New Testament Library. Louisville: Westminster John Knox Press, 2021.

Evans, Craig A., and Stanley E. Porter. *Dictionary of New Testament Background*. Downers Grove: IVP Academic, 2000.

Keener, Craig S. *IVP Bible Background Commentary: New Testament.* 2nd ed. IVP Bible Background Commentary. Downers Grove: IVP Academic, 2014.

King, Philip J., and Lawrence E. Stager. *Life In Biblical Israel.* Louisville: John Knox Press, 2001.

MacArthur, John. *Matthew 16–23 MacArthur New Testament Commentary.* The MacArthur New Testament Commentary. Chicago: Moody Publishers, 1988.

Phillips, John. *Exploring the Gospel of Matthew.* The John Phillips Commentary Series. Grand Rapids: Kregel Publications, 1999.

www.ingramcontent.com/pod-product-compliance
Lightning Source LLC
LaVergne TN
LVHW051655080426
835511LV00017B/2581